A History of Colors

Manlio Brusatin

Translated by
Robert H. Hopcke *and* Paul Schwartz

SHAMBHALA
Boston and London
1991

Shambhala Publications, Inc.
Horticultural Hall
300 Massachusetts Avenue
Boston, Massachusetts 02115

Shambhala Publications, Inc.
Random Century House
20 Vauxhall Bridge Road
London SW1V 2SA

A History of Colors is a translation of *Storia dei colori,*
© 1983 Giulio Einaudi editore s.p.a., Torino
Translation © 1991 by Shambhala Publications, Inc.

9 8 7 6 5 4 3 2 1

First Edition
Printed in the United States of America on acid-free paper
Distributed in the United States by Random House, Inc.,
in Canada by Random House of Canada Ltd, and in
the United Kingdom by the Random Century Group

Library of Congress Cataloging-in-Publication Data

Brusatin, Manlio, 1943–
[Storia dei colori. English]
A history of colors/ Manlio Brusatin; translated by
Robert H. Hopcke and Paul Schwartz.—1st ed.
p.   cm.
Translation of: Storia dei colori.   Includes bibliographical references.
ISBN 0-87773-524-7 (pbk.: acid-free)
1. Color—History.   I. Title.
QC494.7.B7813 1991   90-53584
535.6'09—dc20   CIP

ONE DAY, a young boy met a fairy and asked her if she could satisfy his every wish. "Yes," the fairy answered, "but on one condition. You must never think of the color sea green."

"Is that all?" asked the boy, already sure he was on his way to happiness.

"That's enough!" said the fairy, and with that she disappeared.

But then something strange started happening. No matter how hard he tried, the boy was unable to get the color sea green out of his mind. Time passed, and not only did his various wishes not come to pass, but his life became more and more impossible, until finally, now grown, he seemed simply to wander the world, seized by desperation, convinced that he had been the victim of an evil spell.

CONTENTS

vii

A History of Colors

INTRODUCTION

THE UNIVERSE OF COLORS is a little jewel box of images, a place where Newton built his theory of modern physics with sunlight and certainty, where Goethe in turn constructed an entire history to enshrine a principle he had sought after madly—namely, the unpredictability of nature and the natural simplicity of the arts, of knowing how to see and feel. We should not therefore find it strange that Goethe's first observations on colors, upon which he would later construct his theory, were formed in risky and dangerous circumstances, during the French Revolutionary Wars. Goethe was constrained to observe the play of colors in the clear water of wells along the route of the Prussian military advancement, waters superficially disturbed by the ever-present accidents of war and yet whose purity of reflection remained essentially untouched by the conflict around him.

But what has science proposed concerning this universe of colors? It has determined the seven fundamental colors of the spectrum and has recombined them into the single nonpositive color of their range: white. It has then reduced these fundamental colors from seven to three, instituting a principle of original composition: from three colors (yellow, red, blue) are born all the others, but perhaps only two are truly essential, as some theorists assert. Every theory argues its own presuppositions, and with these it paints the world.

I

Introduction

Our fleeting, sensory perception of colors has linked them, from Leonardo da Vinci to Goethe, to either light or shadow, to primal phenomena seen as producing or absorbing colors, among them the two colors revealed by these perceptions: blue (shadow) and yellow (light), giving rise to the concepts of transparency and proximity, opacity and distance. These principles also regulate degrees of brilliance (brightness) or intensity (saturation) of colors as well as tonality (hue), the principle of their similarity or difference: red, orange, yellow, green, blue, indigo, violet. Moreover, these organizing concepts of light and dark, when applied to the gradations of the various colors, have become part of common speech and are treated as certainties, however relative they may actually be. Even ideas seem opaque or overly clear (in some obscure way) when their prophetic madness shows forth in art or in life.

That a color tends toward wholeness as it tends toward simplicity seems both a necessary and reasonable proposition, which thus reduces the scheme to three fundamental colors. It seems equally well founded to posit that for each color there exists a complementary and contrasting color, a principle that appears when something seems to be "missing" and yet, at the same time, suggests a value indicating precisely what is lacking. So develops a principle of integration and juxtaposition: just as yellow and violet, red and green, blue and orange conflict with each other, they also complete each other. For example, we cannot describe something as "yellow-violet" or "green-red" or "orange-blue" but can indeed describe colors like "blue-green" or "yellow-green," "orange-yellow" or "red-orange," "violet-red" or "blue-violet." "Clear things arise from dark fields," just as dark colors, in keeping with this principle of contrast and complementarity, intuitively arise between the bright, light tints: fishermen attach black flags to their traps so they can see them in the midst of the glimmering sea. Such basic considerations are the foundation for a psychology of perception, beginning with Leonardo's observations and his "perspective of colors," which was introduced as theoretical support for his rebellious experimentation.

These dialectical laws of colors almost always result in a triangular process, in which the passage from light to dark or dark to light (yellow to blue or blue to yellow) produces a color that is different with respect to the first two but that is perhaps the most common in nature—green, nature's true color—a fact that explains the appearance of the two principles governing every tint, shadow (blue) and light (yellow). Because colors are subject to the laws of recall and the ordering principles of memory, they are resolved, by necessity, through a triangular structure in which similarity and opposition result in an interpretive synthesis.

Colors are frequently compared to sounds through the principle of aggregation and composition, but we should also compare them to perfumes and other smells that are simultaneously stimulus and sensation. Such perceptions heighten the flow of memory throughout the body that feels them, like thrills and memories. Sounds also stimulate the memory, but they seem to do so in the direction of self-cancellation, toward silence, by way of a spiral of nostalgia and passive recollection. Music is precisely this silence interrupted, a silence made distinct and separated into geometric harmonies by sound, whereas color produces and creates the thrilling sensation of breath, rising and swelling like a flame. Odors evoke intense but instantaneous pleasure and are connected to the perceptual organs of the nasal area and to our secretory organs, those appendages and conduits of generativity through which pass unknown substances, mucilaginous spurtings, and repulsive wastes. Nevertheless, these organs are the stations of odors, as the camera obscura is for colors. Sounds, however, are almost always (and sometimes overly) respected as functions of the intellect. They enter through a secondary and lateral part of the brain's structure, but seem to penetrate more deeply than that, insinuating themselves inside us, often with the decisiveness of a catastrophe. Philosophers value them highly, placing them high on their scale of values and thus diminishing the virtues of colors, which, in general, they appreciate in a measured way but whose fascination and obscure truth they nevertheless reject.

Sounds reveal a passage of time, an intensity, a timbre; colors a darkness, a clarity, a tone. Timbres and tones may possibly bear a resemblance to each other, but beyond these, sounds seem to fly away (reverberate) into the dimension of space, which contains them, whereas colors move through the dimension of time, which keeps or consumes them. We are pushed toward the colors of our memories as toward the resonances of places we have known. Timbres reveal the nature of the instruments that produce them and evoke shrill colors, drawn together out of contrast, unmediated by half-tones or harmonized colors, like the chords that human voices give to a melody versus the harmony produced by musical instruments.

On the other hand, I believe that colors express altogether vital functions of human existence but do not belong, in general, to the pompous mechanics of the human heart. They belong rather to something more like breathing or the softer organs, which sustain life in a way nearly invisible from the primary bodily functions, not unlike our sense of taste, which provides indirectly for our body's somewhat less obvious signs of life: the growth of hair, the healing of wounds, the flow of blood in the capillaries, the purifications and secretions of digestion, the distillation of blood.

In this sense, colors and tastes are sensations that are relative and reflected, whereas sounds and smells are immediate and unreflective. Between these wax and wane our aspirations and desires, our tastes and our memories, our fate and our nostalgia. With each of these our actions and passions follow their course.

Does a science of color exist? What has existed is a technical desire to create a scientific theory of physical perception. But the two sides from which the analysis arose (object and subject, physical and psychological colors) became conventions within the context of a larger discourse or within a more narrow codification of thought, from which emerge, now and then, glimmers of light.

In fact, the field of colors is a territory with ragged borders located somewhere between the sciences and the arts, between physics and psychology, a land whose configuration constitutes a border between these two diverse cultures. As a result, however, ideas from each side become cloudy and appear easy targets for the other, a region of facile conquest not yet wholly ruled by analytic or experimental methods. Every scientist-philosopher has stopped to consider colors with a certain amount of suspicion; colors have represented change, seduction, untruth, unexpected contrary phenomena and irrevocability, but also suddenness and fate (Eros, remember, is born of Iris). Colors are not in fact corporeal, not alive, not precisely a law of that nature of which they themselves are a reflection of an abstraction; for philosophers, they are something artificial within something natural—"forms," of a sort.

From a biological standpoint nature is colorless, and only in its insistent appearance to humans and insects are its colors revealed, so as to trick those creatures into obeying the law of reproduction. But the law of reproduction is lack of will itself, a participation in the creation of life that does not even require an awareness of the meaning of life—as with the simple, useless words of our everyday conversations, an effortless continuation of life rather than a relentless march toward death.

Insects—creatures that seem sometimes to be all eyes, nothing but chromatic perception—seem to multiply colors according to the laws of their individual species, but their competitive economies, so to speak, are actually more simple. They use these moments of chromatic competition within their color-filled days to carry out their functions, living in color before being continuously, incessantly devoured or created anew in the form of other minuscule living beings. To believe in colors from this standpoint might mean dissolution into the dust of new lives, desires, and passions, endless disappearance and reappearance, on and on without end. Colors thus constitute the most serious deception, an adventure in dust and the habitual pain of living. For this reason, the Italian writers of the sixteenth century amused themselves by recording the "manners" of colors using brief fables told in verse for use by lovers, to make one's love known to another, to defend it or to ransom it like a hostage, to send it forth or to attack it like a sickness.

In this brief history, we will be noting how much actually is derived from the material aspects of colors, the mode of their manufacture, their use and the fate of these colors, up until the tragic beginning of the industrial age, tracing a history from natural dyes subject to the fading of time and the violet-colored ghosts they leave behind, to strong chemical dyes as violent and basic as poison. Beyond this line of inquiry, this will be a story with many fleeting events, wherein we will draw close to the production of ancient marvels so near themselves to the body and yet not to be confused with mere corporeality, a time capable of caring for the art of knowing, without feeling either the weight or the space of it.

This book is dedicated to the rebirth of painting.

1

Sense and Body in Colors

LIKE FISH, REPTILES, BIRDS, and certain hardworking, short-lived insects such as bees and dragonflies, but unlike most other mammals, human beings see in color. This unusual variation has given rise to various theories concerning the nature and perception of colors, particularly the inconsistency of their appearance, their order, and their uselessness.

Sir Isaac Newton, in his *Optiks* (1704), created a foundation for a scientific view of colors "with a solid and coherent theory founded upon such experience which will explain all the phenomena" by way of a principle of absolute physicality, taking very seriously such simple, impressive, and well-observed phenomena as the rainbow, reflections in crystal bowls, and soap bubbles. Everything having to do with transparent bodies was linked to the single phenomenon of the refraction of light and to the rather picturesque categorization of the spectrum (red, orange, yellow, green, blue, indigo, and violet) that would become Newton's turning wheel.[1] Then came red, green, and blue or violet—the three physiological colors of Thomas Young (1773–1829), taking his lead from Hermann von Helmholtz and creating a simplified system that by itself made possible color reproduction. The honor of being a primary color had been alternately denied and be-

9

stowed upon yellow, but in the end, a chromatic alphabet was universally accepted: the three primary colors were sufficient to produce all others. It could be argued that this idea, despite a certain amount of shading here and there, lies at the heart of the technical reproduction of colors and of the prevailing view, which emerged in the last two centuries, of the human eye as perceptually trichromatic. Such a view developed precisely by abbreviating and establishing the range of colors with respect to the many objects and vehicles of their transmission (from photography to television). Compared to the production of colors in ancient times, based as it was upon such fundamental ideas as essences and fixation, modern colors are understood by way of concepts, such as addition and subtraction, that move away from permanence and toward absolute multiplicity and variation.

Despite the modest hegemony enjoyed by the applied sciences and the various revolutionary assaults carried out by modern artists upon the status quo, the domain of colors, long a field of heated philosophical-scientific battles, now seems more like a flooded cave with pockets of accumulated detritus and abandoned materials strewn beside all the strata of natural history, all the fossils and organic matter that form the ground upon which the structures of two different cultures have been built. From Aristotle through Descartes and up to the Enlightenment thinkers who proposed an open system of suggestion and perception, the material aspect of colors has been linked to many areas of philosophical discourse, for example, origin, quality, sensation, interpretation, and truth.

But, Goethe said, every philosopher sees red when he hears talk of colors. Color has always seemed to be the primary explanation of phenomena at the same time as it is discounted as a falsification within interpretative discourse. Colorful speech calls to mind those truths that arise from things in themselves, and yet, to imbue our arguments with color has led, since the time of the Sophists, to inconsistent images, to the oblique suggestion of syllogism, an attempt at deception. Painting and drawing have played opposing roles throughout the history of the visual arts, representing at various times freedom and desire (*libertas*), at others necessity and construction (*obsequium*).

Those who have loosened and overcome the knot between words and things (aphasics) have tried, unsuccessfully, to untangle the skeins of colors. For this reason, a perceptual analysis of colors has gradually brought to light only a few discrete crystals of insight among the diverse cultural materials responsible for this tangle and has done so using a simplification that has made our perception of light somewhat more objective. This simplification is the mechanical model of the eye, a necessary convention for understanding vision. But even with respect to the material elaboration of the first artistic products, there is a tendency to limit primitive colors to three: white, black, and ochre, with white apparently produced through the mixture of lime and chalk, black through charcoal, and yellow-red through clay and ferruginous earth. Yet this primitive trichromatic system, an operational schema suggested by ethnological research, is but a reduced version of a scientific model centered on those three primary colors—colors, incidentally, whose wavelengths are so close as to appear almost irrelevant to the objects that bear them. The truth is that the different corpus of colors, whether primitive or civilized, still must be seen in comparison to and in juxtaposition with the extended range of objects that (through the rules of perceptual and visual technical production) constitute a group's or society's way of life: one need only think of the hundreds of reds seen by the Maori, the seven types of white seen by Eskimos, or the hundred or more shades of gray perceived by twentieth-century urban Europeans.

Some recent linguistic analyses have isolated within various language families the generative principles for a language of color and have begun to include the idea of "terms of classification" proper to each original language (that is, in languages where a more abstract normative schema at odds with true chromatic perception does not exist). With this development we have begun to ignore and thus to lose the most elementary and intuitive forms of chromatic perception, like hue (a dominant color with respect to groups of comparative colored material), brightness (the luster or amount of light associated with a shaded or faded tint), and saturation (the precise, full tone of colors that bring to mind a greater intensity or purity of material). All these represent a nonreductive discourse concerning the production of color within the still-unreduced bounds of the archaic or primitive world, where it is still impossible to connect color with a principle of unity or uniformity, with a chromatic direction. Despite this, it is possible to suggest a rather esoteric schema that includes a kind of evolution in the perception of color throughout the wide range of color production among various human civilizations. The following diagram, read from left to right, proceeds according to a principle of expansion that starts with two fundamental colors (white and black), which evolve through juxtaposition and differentiation from the one color that, in every civilization, is born originally from blood and the life it carries: red.[2]

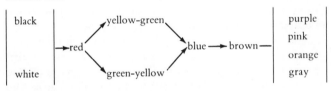

Ulterior proof for the uniformity of this mechanistic, reductive analysis can be found by comparing a modern list of colors with the "language of colors" derived, for example, from Homeric poetry. The latter generally evokes a world of fleeting appearances, in which simple combinations of colors throughout the spectrum reveal a chromatic essence, and encapsulates the way that Western history consists of a continuous attempt at recovering the classical past in the face of abandonment, mystery, and loss. The analogy, however insignificant, between these five classical shades and the other (seven) of our own chromatic culture, invented by Newton, makes intuitive sense: *leukos* (white), *glaukos* (gray), *erythros* (red), *chloros* (green), *kuanos* (translated as "blue"): with a similar lack of nonidentity, other shades are lacking.

The most important catalogue of the world of ancient colors is Eugene Chevreul's *Des couleurs and de leurs applications aux arts industriels* (On colors and their applications in the industrial arts), an encyclopedia of 14,400 chromatic tones published in 1864, before the proliferation of such newer synthetic coloring agents as aniline, malveine, alizarine, fucsine, and metilene, products of the nineteenth-century chemical industry. That industry, capable of producing the full spectrum of purple-red and dark blue dyes commonly in use, thus eliminated the cultivation of those plants that had until then supplied the necessary dyestuff, such as madder (*Rubia tinctorum*) or woad (*Isatis tinctoria*), plants that became little more than botanical curiosities and that bequeathed to the regions and fields of their former cultivation names indicating their use in the ancient dye industry. Beside listing every possible shade, Chevreul acted in accordance with Newton's chromatic sensibilities, insisting upon the empirical harmony of a juxtaposition of colors in his famous *cercles chromatiques* (whose reproduction for the 1855 edition, printed using the chromolithographic system, was quite a challenge), and this model is often cited as the theoretical basis for impressionistic and pointillistic painting, as appears later in the works of the American Ogden Rood (1879). Chevreul's simpler and more synthetic tendencies became evident in a method he himself described as "experimental a posteriori," by which, in a new, more positive spirit and yet in a still decidedly Enlightenment manner, he intended to (1) define colors; (2) define their mixtures, and (3) define the effects of their contrasts.[3]

In the latter half of the nineteenth century, all systematic research on color was based on the modern arrangement of colored objects while at the same time working to expand the outer limits of industrial production and diffusion. The experience of color created by the emerging chemical industry obliterated the previous experiences of colors that, since ancient times, were created through secret dye mixtures using plants and insects of a particular locality—mixtures whose quality depended upon the length of time taken to produce them. Here instead, within the same coloring agent, a progressive, accelerated application of technology was combined with a fairly primitive grade of color exclusively in the range of red and blue. Alongside the leveling effect of industrial dyes, out of the depths of memory, as if to resist all mechanically produced colors, was born the *colore estetico*, a cultivated appreciation and attention toward lost colors, attenuated shades faded through use and observation, the patinas of time: true "primitive" colors of an ancient age, recreated by turning modern fantasies upside down.

In fact, our visual perception nowadays appears based on a split brain and seems focused upon two fundamental colors: red and blue, with centrifugal action intuitively and schematically associated with red and centripetal action associated with blue (likewise with hot and cold colors, which also refer to these two dominant shades). Unconsciously this evokes the primordial symbolic juxtaposition of blue as a Uranian, masculine color and red as a chthonic, feminine color, even though this seems generally a case of what De Rochas termed "extériorisation de la sensibilité": in irrationally enlarging these original contrasts, we can only admit to how arbitrary it is to make distinctions among the enormous mass of meanings contained within the universe of colors. Generally speaking, meanings, like colors, express neither truth nor value if they are separated from the various modes in which they are "given" or "taken away." These modes are connected to forms, to techniques, to the manual history of production, to manifestations of perceptions in which all originality or primitiveness is intuited within the flux of subjects seen *against* objects, of objects *above* subjects, which cannot be compared to a body of work within disciplines produced in other times and places. All scientific reductions, all artificial productions in the chromatic universe are inevitably set apart from the truth of technique alone, which by itself manufactured the very chromatic universe that informs (through similarities or declarations) such applied scientific observations themselves.

In practice, colors subsist in a relationship of simple correspondence or cause, connecting how they are seen with how they are produced, after which they may distinguish themselves through the fragmentation of survival, resistance, or eruption, which are like historic waves of exaltation, overflowing color. For this reason we should not be deluded into thinking that colors, for all their apparent flexibility in every language and every schema, can be easily fitted into our perfect semantic system of color = function = emotion seemingly confirmed by the naive games of perceptual psychology or, worse, by the useless duplication of archival collectionism, a catalogue of shades broken down into an identifying scale of colors.

Within this lack of unity, color becomes, in equal measure, not only a logical process wherein material density is subtracted as part of a material technique of "objectification," but also as a process wherein a superficial idea and a curative tint are added together upon a reality which we understand through reality. Color defines every material field of endeavor and every ideological history, but it does so irregularly, demarcating in this fashion areas of discontinuity, placing in front of every viewer and every perceptual analyst principles unabstracted from place, topographies of reference, sensations of pause, unexpected open spaces in the course of a trip through the woods, memories of peoples and places left behind. This fact thus creates a science predisposed to speak of the fantastic existence of color only in the most diffuse way, until such time as color can be detached from the things that carry it and from the colorful conversations and feelings that define it, treating it as an emission of energy invisible to the human eye capable of perceiving only certain well-known frequencies: colors as Rimbaud's "naissances latentes" and "golfes d'ombres." One ought not forget that there exists a material, cultural history of colors, which through relationships of economic dependency brought about a confrontation between civilizations that had previously communicated through the single rare medium of spices, in the markets of

17

Asia and the Americas: China black and black dust, the translucent colors of lacquers, as well as the indigo leaves of the Antilles and the cochineal of Central America, vivid red brazilwood together with the "precious colors" of gemstones and metals, desired for the brilliance of their splendid substance.

In general, color is almost always contrasted with form, as if it were an extremely fine material. This contrast can function to verify one's subjective judgment of what is real and at the same time to establish a rule (the chromatic spectrum) as a synthesis and objectification of reality. The former position gives rise to colors often termed "physiological" but that could also be termed "psychological" (not "perceptual," strictly speaking, but rather "perceptionistic"), while the latter gives rise to colors termed, rather inappropriately, "physical," but also called "subjective" with reference to the subject (animal, machine, substance) that perceives and reacts to chromatic impressions. Every science, technology, or psychology of vision always has the intention of filtering and reorganizing each image and manifestation of the visible world with interpretations that are "more real" by way of many different versions of colors, a process that ends up abstracting the physical from lived experience, making colors appear rather like cultural artifacts such as the stories depicted in paintings, printing, photography, or film, rather than creating an independent, and useless, history of colors above all other visual representations or communications. These unevocative, monochromatic operations regard the arts as ingenuous productions that exist in some radical way apart from any artistic aspirations, which avail themselves of pure color (from impressionist to action painting), pure exaltations of one's own figurative program, now that form has been eliminated.

But before allowing ourselves any reductionistic exaltations of color, we should consider the predialectic classification Johann Wolfgang von Goethe presented in his *Farbenlehre* (1808–10): *physiological colors* (elsewhere called casual, imaginary, fantastic, accidental, apparent, fleeting, spectral); *physical colors* (also called apparent, fleeting, false, variable, specious, emphatic, fantastic); and *chemical colors* (recognized as material, corporeal, fixed, permanent, substantial, true). Precisely because of the attempt to distinguish between objectivity and subjectivity in judging the first two categories, the denominations seem to overlap and the nomenclature seems confused. Physical colors seize upon a single image for their infrequent appearance, physiological colors evoke their logical complements through the colors of physical pathology and color blindness, and chemical colors suddenly reveal the hopes of a blind science, still in its infancy, faced with a great artistic tradition then at its end. Is the perception of color one of pure sensation and vibration, where cause prevails over effect, as in Newton's theory, or rather, is it the result of sensibility and intellectual action through retinal perception of intensity, extension, and quality, as Schopenhauer suggested? Thus one swings on a polarity around which theorists improvised a spectrum as well as all the similarities and differences of the various disciplines.

A History of Colors

Discourse on color has always been linked to the observation of objects in light, along with a consideration of light's disappearance or fading. This creates two different senses of colors: first, color as material; second, color as sensation and sign. To denote this distinction, we will use the adjective *coloristic* for the first case, referring to corporeality and matter, and *chromatic* for the second, referring to the phenomena of perception and suggestion, without distinguishing perceiver from perceived in the flow of color that unites the two. Instead of this distinction, we will speak of the reciprocal, interchangeable value of colors that can either intensify or mute, a value that derives from the confounding of those two functions. Thus, we will investigate how they work or do not work and where their identity splits and multiplicity is attenuated, where the line of shadow becomes the appearance of color, its mechanism of illumination.

2

Color as Figure and Fate

EGYPTIAN TABLETS and writings concerning colors are based on a principle that uses hard stones such as granite and marble as points of reference, thus creating a symbol that profoundly informs the painting of the region. Both Egyptians and Jews dressed their priests in white, the latter equating the various levels of moral conduct expected of their priests with precious gems, the colors of these gems associated exclusively with the twelve tribes of Israel: sardonyx (red) associated with courage; emerald (green) with curative powers; topaz (yellow) with gentleness; carbuncle/garnet (orange) with the force of life; jasper (dark green) with fertility; sapphire (blue) with purity; zircon (purple) with strength; amethyst (violet) with relief of sadness; agate (pearl gray) with happiness; chrysolite (golden yellow) with protection against envy; beryl (azure) with calmness; onyx (pink) with chastity.

Among the various coloring materials available to the Egyptians were *khesebedh* (lapis lazuli, blue), *khenemet* (ruby, red), *nesemet* (azure), *mefekat* (emerald, green) and *kem* (dark brown), which constitute a corporeal coloristic group that Rummel (1870) used, by analogy, for his principle of cosmetics: "White corrects the skin tone, red freshens the color of the cheeks, azure underscores the line of the forehead, carmine livens the color of the lips, henna (light red) dips the fingers in the light of dawn."[1] In addition to these colors of seduction, one might add those widely used cosmetic preparations that enabled one to present oneself to the gods of the underworld and that substituted for the color of life: black (*semeti*) and green (*uadh*).

The principles by which color is used on the body can be discerned even in nature. For example, we could term tonalities of red (cock's comb, tongue, genitals) "manifest" or "conative" signals. Such striking colors create an appearance or display that produces attraction, attention, wonder, desire for contact or flight, standoff, sexual exhibition, temptation, exploration, all of which are heightened by the use of colors that intensify or camouflage the mouth, fingers, nipples, earlobes, nostrils, cheeks, buttocks, labia, or penis.

Other colors one could call—solely on the basis of physiological perceptions—"latent" or "emotional," as with dark blue or green, whose virtue is an ability to hide and reveal, to unite while simultaneously delimiting one's territory or home. These are "pregnant" colors, emblems of possessing and belonging, reinforced in the acts of carrying or conferring. The dark blue ink of tattoos has a double purpose, distinguishing the bearer from the environment as well as distinguishing him as part of a species or group. To be truly human means to be painted, and whoever simply maintains his own skin intact is really no different from an animal, indistinguishable from the rest of humanity and all other visible creatures, an outsider to the group and the in-circle of the village: he "does not belong."[2] This work of pictorial surgery, this justifiable, man-made torture, thus grafts upon the human body a different sort of skin, which becomes a part of it, like one's culture or one's fate. In this way, the various blues of the tattoo artist flow over the energetic reds of blood and fire like the natural waters of life, gathering and protecting these life forces from sudden dispersal onto the bodies of other subjects: however dissimilar and conflictual the connection, life and art, colors and color, remain inseparable.

According to Hebrew tradition, the name of the first man, Adam, means "red" and "alive," and still today, in languages of the Slavic family red denotes "living," "beautiful." Given the abstract, immaterial origins of white and black from light and shadow, the colors associated with primordial chaos, with priest and prophets, red—the color of blood and life—represents the most effective agent for banishing the pallor of death and for honoring the living memory of the departed. Chinese vases, colored oxblood red and originating in rites of sacrifice, are a sign for the living and take the place of the individual whose "shadow is colored with red." Like the humors of his body, they represent what is common among the living, a shell in some way carried through life that now, in death, lies red and empty.

Colors like yellow, orange, and white, with their extraverted, one could say "manifestational," qualities, can function to exorcise or forbid that which is unacceptable, indicating what is prohibited or revered, and in this way may participate in the same realm of intangible reality as priests,

prophets and hermaphrodites (who were sometimes albino).
Likewise, other colors could be included in the broad category
of "latent" colors, such as black or violet (in general the dark
color of ashes), and may indicate the timeless existence of
those belonging to a particular community. While members
of a privileged inner circle are marked by their own "distinctive" colors, black and violet clearly indicate an individual's
marginality within a social group, as in the case of illness,
widowhood, slavery, or treason. All of these have their own
rituals of rehabilitation and re-inclusion, usually involving
atonement and redemption, which, if not performed properly, may lead to eternal ostracism. The coloring of skin has
long been a custom indicating such exclusion, and one might
even go so far as to say that such distinctive social structures
are organized according to color, as in the castes (*varna*) of
Indian society.

In Greece, whose civilization acts as lens through which all
of Western culture must be viewed, the use of colors to mark
social respect or suspicion was even more prominent.
Pythagoreans had a notable disdain for color, considering it
something extrinsic—revelatory at times, certainly, but
epiphenomenal. This attitude seems to have determined the
dominant approach taken by science in examining the nature
of color, with principles that negated or resolved the significance of color in favor of numerical analogues. Against the
Pythagoreans, Empedocles considered color the soul of life
and the root of all existence (earth, air, fire, and water, represented by yellow, black, red and white, respectively),

whereas Democritus confined himself to observing the dialectic relationship of white and black, which seemed to alternate and even at times become confused with each other. The Stoics and Epicureans at times minimized, at times appreciated the effect that color plays in the realm of sensation and in the ordering of rational thought. As Mario Equicola comments:

> One sees how difficult it is to speak of colors and the dangers one runs when one wishes to use the ancient vocabulary in reference to our own commonplace terms. Some philosophers thought the air and water white, fire red, earth black: Astrologers called Saturn brown, Jupiter blue, Mars red, yellow the Sun, green Venus, ashen Mercury, white the Moon. Others bestowed the colors upon them otherwise, Saturn black, Jupiter green, white Venus, variegated Mercury, yellow the Moon, and on Mars and the Sun all are in agreement: The meanings of colors for Italians, Spaniards, and French vary in certain places.[3]

The first comprehensive system of thought on the nature of color was elaborated using the teachings of Aristotle—that is, if the brief treatise *On Colors*, first published in 1497, can be attributed to him. A more likely attribution, however, would be to place it among the various physical-practical researches of Aristotle's disciple Theophrastus, halfway between *On Sensation* and the *History of Plants* and roughly coincident with *On Odors*. This is more or less toward the end of Theophrastus's phase of philosophical uncertainty concerning color (*chroma*) present both in the theory of atomism, due to the absence of materiality in color, as well in Platonic theory, where color's quasi-materiality interfered with the ideal opposition between light and shadow.

Theophrastus's pointedly naturalistic synthesis was applied, without distinction, to every surface or "skin," whether painted, colored, or natural (*chromata*); to powders and pigments (*pharmaka*); and to other cosmetics and lotions, roots, and other essences used for dyeing. Nevertheless, it ignores the chromatic limit represented by the color blue, leading one to speculate that the Greeks were blind to this particular color. Friedrich Nietzsche observed:

> How different nature must have appeared to the Greeks if, as we have to admit, their eyes were blind to blue and green, and instead of the former saw deep brown, instead of the latter yellow (so that they used the same word, for example, to describe the colour of dark hair, that of the cornflower, and that of the southern sea; and again the same word for the colour of the greenest plants and that of the human skin, honey, and yellow resins: it has been shown that their greatest painters reproduced their world using only black, white, red and yellow)— how different and how much more like mankind nature must have appeared to them, since in their eyes the coloration of mankind also preponderated in nature and the latter as it were floated in the atmosphere of human coloration! (Blue and green dehumanise nature more than anything else does:) It is on this *deficiency* that there grew up in the Greeks the playful facility which distinguished them for seeing natural events as gods and

demi-gods, that is to say as human-like forms.—But let this be no more than a metaphor for a further supposition. Every thinker paints his world in fewer colours than *are actually there*, and is blind to certain individual colours. This is not merely a deficiency. By virtue of this approximation and simplification he introduces harmonies of colours *into the things themselves*, and these harmonies possess great charm and can constitute an enrichment of nature. Perhaps it was only in this way that mankind first learned to take *pleasure* in the sight of existence: existence, that is to say, was in the first instance presented to them in one or two colours, and thus present harmoniously: mankind then as it were practised on these few shades before being able to go over to several. And even today many an individual works himself out of a partial colour-blindness into a rich seeing and distinguishing but is also *obliged to give up and relinquish* some of his earlier ones.[4]

Color as a mythological figure appears, first of all, in Iris, the personification of the rainbow as message from the gods and the original breath of Eros.[5] But Senophanes of Colophon sees only three colors in this phenomenon, purple, red, and yellow-green. Darkness and shadow are treated as if they are by nature inimical to color, similar to black: according to classicists and romantics, death for the Greeks was indicated by a deep blue, the color of the Attic sky, which extinguishes every other color and which, like bad news, is not to be named. The esteem accorded to Attic yellow and Sinopian red in classical poetry made these the material counterparts of earth and fire, "ripening" substances in a complementary and reciprocal relationship to each other. These were opposed to water, whose clarity was always associated with white (in mythology, fresh water was created before salt water), and to air, which in Empedocles' philosophy was black as the night and held within it both primordial chaos and the miraculous creation of the world. Blown down from on high, revivifying the ashen remains of combustion, air moves earth, which holds water, which puts out fire, which heats and lifts air (a cycle of black-yellow, yellow-white, white-red, red-yellow, yellow-black).

We do not know why the Greeks and their aesthetic sensibilities excluded the color blue, given its presence in the nearby Assyrian-Chaldean civilizations, as evidenced by the use of cobalt oxides in their ceramic ware, as well as in the so-called fried ware of ancient Egypt, which consisted of a colored mixture of sand, copper filings, and sodium carbonate baked in an oven. Before any cultural intermixing, azure-blue already had a distinctly mixed, oriental character, representing a shadowy sort of illumination, especially with regard to the materialistic foundations of Western thought, with its distinction between the world of ideas and the world of being (white and black), as well as between nature and substance (yellow and red).

Even in Homeric poems, blue does not appear: Athena's common epithet, *glaukopis*, is taken to mean "owl-eyed," that is, able to see and be seen at night, just as later the nocturnal bird was adopted as a symbol of Athens's genius. The adjective *kuanos* (in Latin *caeruleus*) actually connotes the dark-green tone of the sea reflecting the sky at times when the water does not have that darker, more threatening Homeric color to it: *oinopos*, the color of wine. In Homer, the purple color of woolen robes abounds in the *Iliad*, while in the *Odyssey* household furnishings appear in a more stylish red, derived from the leaves and root of Anatolian madder (*erythrodamos*) or, more probably, from *chermes*, a crimson-red cochineal dye imported from Lydia about which most classical authors knew very little: they seem to have thought that it was derived from the fruit of a small plant, whereas in reality, it came from colonies of minuscule, parasitical insects (*Coccus ilicis*) living in holm oaks whose bodies were gathered and dried to create the dye.

The combat uniform of the Spartan army was made of red wool dyed with madder, along with shoes in red leather similar to those produced in the city of Amiclea, known throughout the Mediterranean world for leather craftsmanship on a par with that of Morocco. In Athens, the dye shop (*ergasterion*) needed abundant water and fuel for boiling fabrics in fixatives and dyes, but began to be looked upon as an unclean trade, like that of the tanner, and thus was consigned to the outer limits of the city. The Attic dye shop developed from the beginning the technique of printing fabric with designs and figures in two major colors (red and black). With the dyeing of thread, multicolor fabrics woven with a mixture of these dominant colors came into favor, such that the production of such fabric was fairly common to the light industry carried out in women's domestic quarters.

Despite Theophrastus's testimony to the contrary, the rare qualities of pastel were held in esteem. This blue pigment created by grinding *Isatis tinctoria* was, along with the red *Rubia tinctorum*, the most widely used in the dye industry of the time and was occasionally mixed with indigo (*Atramentum indicum*, dark indigo) for blue dyes. However, these colors do not, strictly speaking, belong to the classical Greek tradition but rather appear only intermittently in Alexandria in Egypt through Hellenistic influences by way of Asia Minor.

In *De materia medica*, Pedanius Dioscorides (first century A.D.), following the tradition of Theophrastus, not only supplies galenical remedies but also describes all the various qualities of the plants most widely used to create the bases for dyes—for example, orchil (canary weed), bastard saffron, and oak gall, dyes in the range of red, orange, brown, and yellow, according to the fixative used. This procedure employed mostly fermented urine (from "a young boy" or "a man drunken on strong wine," according to the various formulas passed down from the Middle Ages as trade secrets), and so, obviously, came the trade's reputation of uncleanness, as well as its banishment to the outskirts of the city.

Of all the various theories concerning the nature of color (*chroma* and *pharmakon*), the one formulated by Zeno of Citium and handed down to us by Plutarch—"colors are the primary schema of the material world"—tends to use the concept of chromatic perception in a well-defined way, as something midway between matter and form. Given birth by the father of Stoicism, therefore, this formulation soon was adopted by most of the subsequent Latin writers. Of course, Zeno held his lessons and shaped his philosophy beneath the porticos of Athens decorated with frescoes by Polygnotus, a painter who filled the pure shapes of his figures with typical Attic colors. In Aristotle's judgment, Polygnotus was more endowed philosophically with *ethos* than Zeuxis, with his coloristic affectations, or Apelles, with his sophisticated *a velatura* technique. Only in Polygnotus was painting able to express the sense of revelation and the nobility of matter that so motivated philosophical discourse at the time, and it did this through the deliberate quality of the work and the marriage of color and figure within a specified contour and within a particular tonal range. Color by itself is too easily contaminated by artificial, technical operations, which often seek to evoke from the viewer feelings of seduction, fascination, desire, or possession. These tricks are those of the *sophistes*, originally craftsmen and artists, who, like the sophists after them, taught ways of obscuring the stability of social conditions and the laws that support them under the cloak of ever-changing metaphors so as to secure for oneself a place in society through means other than wisdom or knowledge, firing ambition and wonderment with new words and phrases that, like colors, are but the appearance, rather than the substance, of society. Such nonethical operations were roundly and consistently denounced throughout classical philosophy.

Despite the refutation of the philosophers, however, the Greek world was a major consumer of the social fortune represented by the color purple, which included the personal ambitions of the Sophists. This color, representing fame and wealth, was a decoration for highly placed individuals of state as well as a sign of personal and political productivity. Purple functioned as a symbol of the equality shared, through advantages and rewards, by those in government and those in trade. In fact, Mediterranean culture had been completely overtaken by the red-purple of the Phoenicians, who had, along with their production capacity, the means for a wide distribution of their product. This wonderful dye, extracted in minute quantities from thousands of murices and particular species of saltwater snails (*Murex trunculus, Murex brandaris, Purpura haemastoma*), nevertheless did not reveal its coloring properties until after a drawn-out technical process of washing and boiling the various pieces of wool and then exposing the fabric to the air of the morning sea on the shores of Tyre, which acted to oxidize and fix the color. This ancient color, therefore, can no longer be produced in the modern age. It brings to mind the classical color of the soul, which, according to Virgil, is also purple.[6]

Vitruvius mentions at great length various types of purple, and yet, in consulting the classics, one finds each writer providing different and sometimes contradictory rules for its production. The comparatively recent discovery (at the beginning of our own century) of the actual dyeing process used to produce purple both upsets and puts a fair bit of distance between modern and classical notions concerning this part of the spectrum and the various virtues of violet thread. Purple was still a part of Florentine trade in the sixteenth century due to the red-purple color of that plant widely cultivated and used throughout Europe, madder (or, in Italian, *garanza*, from which comes a word indicating respect for the quality of a product, *garanzia* or guarantee); so we feel hidden within the red-purple of the ancients the commercial secret of popularity, the desire for a good whose only voice is that of the "form" of its color. Here value appears in its original state, far from its monetary counterpart and the commercial, all-consuming lust after cash; here, it is carried by the nature and quality of the object itself, which, revealing artistry never again to be equalled, reveals the soul contained within the feverish work of exchange and demand. The color purple is the "language" of a product transformed by work into art, a language anterior to all the terms of contracts and competition that determine price, a glimpse into another world of technique by way of a seductive, "purple" simplicity. It is exalted as a marvel, the first volley in the game between supply and demand at a time where conventional values or cash equivalencies do not yet contaminate respect for productivity or codify such falsifications of value into contracts for exchange of property. Thus we can distinguish between an authentic manufacture of quality products and the false creation of a purchase price. The aura of goodness (*tantum*) that surrounds purple becomes consumed in trade whenever a monetary relationship (*quantum*) is established with regard to the very material used to produce it, an ever-increasing quantity of shells. The color purple creates all of this (*incantum*) and tends to expand this monetary relationship infinitely, since it can compete in value with gold.

The Phoenician god of dye working, Melcarth, was the patron of a nomadic class of well-educated and inventive artisans, who used their social marginality to emigrate from Crete beginning around 1600 B.C. This migration can be understood in the myth of Daedalus and Icarus, who, exhibiting similar initiative and technique, flouted the rules of production laid down by the royal court and transgressed the imprisoning order of trade manufacturing (represented in the myth by the labyrinth), in which goods take on value solely through decree of the monarch and through his personal use. Once the subordinate relationship between king and court-employed artisans was dissolved and after the downfall of the Minoan dynasty, the Daedalean migrants found themselves uprooted and faced with considerable difficulties and misfortune in their attempts to apply their technical knowledge and continue a tradition of apprenticeship (the loss of the son, Icarus). For this reason, there was no protection against any vengeful persecution that the powers and principalities saw fit to pursue over "beautiful, durable goods" before this ingenious, artistically accomplished class of artisans finally won their freedom (Daedalus's flight and his unremitting pursuit by the emissaries of King Minos until the monarch's violent death, which was arranged by Daedalus himself).

These far-flung groups of tradespeople found themselves in demand in the city of Tyre under the reign of Solomon (950 B.C.) during the construction of the great temple in Jerusalem, as they excelled not only in metallurgy and mechanics but in dye working as well, an art parallel to that of Asclepius in its employment of plants and their essences. Thus, an entire history can be seen through the ethical-social prestige commanded by the rich, incomparable color purple throughout the Mediterranean world, the dominant color in all the more highly developed figurative traditions of the West.

In the areas of weaving, dye working, and other pictorial or metal working arts, Roman civilization drew upon the vast, indigenous tradition of the peninsula and of the Etruscans and emphatically affirmed the importance of the *colos* [sic] *principalis* of the *ars purpuraria*, which had been developed with the supply and storage of luxury goods and products selected from the weavers and dye shops of Greece and Sicily, such as Cibyra, Tarantum, and Syracuse. Among the corporations of the *collegium tinctorum*, wisely favored by Rome's second king, Numa Pompilius, specific professions little by little distinguished themselves according to the production and "color value" of the goods. The dyer's trade continued to be condemned as dirty, base, and degraded, though all the while the excellence of the finished products continued to be praised. The *Aulularia* of Plautus exemplifies the distinctions being made between the various producers and purveyors of dye garments: the *flammarii* (yellow-orange dyes, from safflower), the *crocotarii* (light yellow, from crocus or saffron), the *spadicarii* (brown or rust colors, or dyes derived from tannin), and the several *violarii*, among which were distinguished, for example, the *purpurarii* from the *carinarii*, just as the quality of material dyed with extracts from Phoenician sea snails was distinguished from that derived from Ionian or Tyrrhenian shells. Purple, as *colos principalis*, was used as an index of high appreciation and respect to the point of becoming the *color officialis*, an imperial color used exclusively by the Caesars, as a trademark, so to speak, a patent of the Augustan family. Laws and standards were therefore promulgated to protect the finished product and to regulate dye materials and the choice of wools, as well as the distribution, exchange, and determination of prices throughout the Roman world. After Nero, an even more exclusive monopoly was retained by the person of Severus Alexander to regulate and authorize, within the territories ruled by Rome, the distribution of *officinae purpurariae*, who thus became dependent upon a single center of trade and upon the authority of the capital.

The production of imperial purple lasted quite a long time, even up to the Byzantine purple named "cockroach" for its blood-red, dark violet tone—the only fragments we possess for comparison to modern shades of this color. On the other hand, to get a sense of this final color of the Caesarean era, we are familiar with a very hard stone used exclusively for statues of Caesar: porphyry.

Against the *color officialis* of Imperial Rome's institutions was pitted the barbarian's color, *caeruleus color*, a dark blue derived from woad, identified and translated into Latin as *vitrum* or *glastum* (from the Celtic root *glas*). With woad the Picts of ancient Britain would paint their bodies for battle to appear frightful, a "spectral army" in Tacitus's words. Even in everyday life, the practice of injecting dye beneath the skin of various parts of the body was quite common among the women of ancient Britain, who "went about nude in the colors of Ethiopians," according to Pliny the Elder.

The late Roman period saw the development of a system of contrasting, chromatic signals used to distinguish between factions or parties: the colors of the circus. The introduction of insignias and of red and white banners to the circus came about in order to distinguish between men on foot and men on horseback, and these two colors thus have an association with and stand in opposition to the green and blue used in the favorite of all the circus games, the horse races, where they were employed for their ability to be seen at a distance and thereby differentiate between teams. These various groups would enjoy loyal support from various quarters until the emperor entered in by favoring a particular color or sponsoring the more acclaimed teams in their difficult race against chance. The original assignment of colors to different groups in the circus was later interpreted according to the seasons of the year—the fire of summer, the snow of winter, the green of spring, and the darkness of autumn—or according to the four elements—water, earth, fire and air. The denotation and probable origin for this use of colors was discussed by a number of Latin writers, with Cassiodorus's interpretation of the denotations then current—*russati, albati, prasini*, and *veneti*—most widely known. Yet perhaps the pageantry of the circus made manifest a deeper conflict between Latin colors (light) and bar-

37

baric colors (dark) in the melting pot of the Roman Empire's final days.

The last two of these groupings (*prasini* and *veneti*, or the Greens and the Blues) continued to last beyond the circus and become political parties, supplanting the first two (*russati* and *albati*, or the Reds and the Whites) throughout the reign of Justinian and Theodora, in part because of the way green and blue harked back to the fierce barbarians who wore these colors in the circus and who survived to carry off the carcass of Western civilization after the end of the empire. Theodoric intervened in support of the Greens against the patrician support of the Blues, who were subsequently favored under the Byzantinophile reign of Amalasuntha. In Byzantium, the conflict between the Monophysite color of *prasini* or green and the Orthodox color of *veneti* or turquoise-blue resulted in the explosive revolt at Nika in response to the partiality shown toward the Blues by the emperor Justinian. Such clashes, resulting from underlying ethnic tensions, are the first instances of a political use of color to aid in armed struggle. The Blues dressed as Huns and proclaimed Justinian's humble Orthodox origins by renaming him Upravda, according to Procopius's recollections in *Anecdota*:

> The people had since long previous time been divided, as I have explained elsewhere, into two factions, the Blues and the Greens. Justinian, by joining the former party, which had already shown favor to him, was able to bring everything into confusion and turmoil, and by its power to sink the Roman state to its knees before

him. Not all the Blues were willing to follow his leadership, but there were plenty who were eager for civil war. Yet even these, as the trouble spread, seemed the most prudent of men, for their crimes were less awful than was in their power to commit. Nor did the Green partisans remain quiet, but showed their resentment as violently as they could, though one by one they were continually punished; which, indeed, urged them each time to further recklessness. For men who are wronged are likely to become desperate.[7]

Going beyond this personification of colors as emblems and attending instead to the respective coloring materials used, we see the predominance in ancient Greece of Attic yellow over red being inverted in the Roman world, where red is favored over yellow, at least from what we may glean from authors such as Ovid, Propertius, Seneca, and Pliny, who provide a nearly encyclopedic history of the fortune of red in the West. Precise distinctions are made in these writings between colors that are *naturales* and *artificiales*, with full preference given to those that can be obtained through art and whose appearance transcends the substances from which they are derived. For Vitruvius, for example, in the process of creating colors to be used in painting, recipes are suggested for producing a more sophisticated indigo, a color rare but hardly ignored in the Roman world. That which was still not possible for the dye maker, who was still bound to a tradition and to a single product, became possible in painting, where practical, technical knowledge resulted in an ability to create "beautiful colors" through artifice, resulting in a body of hidden, authentic wisdom that came to belong to the trade of a painter. Thus, problems would arise in the late Middle Ages when the publication and distribution of recipe books would reveal these secrets of the workshops and break the power of the guild laws, creating an atmosphere of public disclosure and free enterprise that would represent the first flowering of Italian humanism.

Nevertheless, since the beginning of Rome, ocher-yellow and its coloring power, drawn from traces of iron in the earth, continued to be used alongside the more dominant red obtained through the baking of earth, a presence strikingly apparent in the effusion of the brick structures that Roman civil engineering erected all over the green of the countryside. Noteworthy, too is the widespread adoption in Roman interiors of the encaustic techniques used in the red plaster of Pompeii. In this way, the baked clay of Etruscan and Roman bricks gained the coloristic upper hand over the light yellow earth and stones of the Greek-Mediterranean world, so that the singled-minded program of urban development carried out by each and every emperor would be, in the words of Suetonius, to "relinquere marmoream urbem quam lateritiam accepisset," that is, to transform the city made of bricks into marble, since republican Rome was a city dominated by terra-cotta red. And yet, despite the monumentality of white and variegated marbles on the facades of monuments dating from imperial times, the fabric of urban life was woven in terra-cotta, in the compact houses, *insulae*, and especially the walls of the city. And this remains the color of the Italian city-state of the Middle Ages. Thus, a program of urban development designed to create the sense of a *compartmentalized* city (divided into blocks) rather than that of an *occupied* city (filled within its walls) would, in general, consist of imposing white marble statuary upon the red of the common people through new monuments to urban life. But in the end, terra-cotta would remain the color of Rome and of Italy because of the dominant red-purple tonality that constitutes the historical and chromatic background of the entire Mediterranean world, from the cosmetic red of the Egyptians to Punic purple.

The triad of material colors (white, red, and black) determines an ongoing relationship of earthly, corporeal values: red, with its fullness of natural abundance, precedes the white (*albus, candidus*) of uncertainty and rarity and is opposed to the black (*ater*) of slavery and ill omen. Artemidorus Daldianus (second century C.E.), in his *Oneirocritica* (Interpretation of dreams), declares that the appearance of red clothes is a sure sign of good fortune and fame; white clothes, in which the dead are buried, instead are a sign of great calamity, while black, the symbol of mourning that distinguishes the surviving family from the deceased, may indicate in a dream only minor misfortunes. After assigning the classical values to red, white and black, Artemidorus mentions a less obvious color of emotion: violet, the shade of separation, a sign of detachment and widowhood, which subsequently will become the color of fasting and prayer for the Catholic church, as it arises

from the militant, antiheretical nucleus created with the Ni-
caean council in 325 C.E.

In Christianity, violet drives out the purple-red of the pagan world and is the sign of the temporary death that occurs
in a state of sin while awaiting baptism and pentitential liber-
ation. Alongside and opposite it is the green of new life, a life
informed by *naturaliter christiana*, a practice organized according to wisdom and stewardship in both dress and laws. Green
is the preeminent color of Christianity, associated with the
Eucharistic love feast, *agape*, along with the sacramental white
of communion and the white robe of the neophyte. Green
accompanies the pastoral mission of the Church and its sac-
raments for the living and the pure of heart (and not those
connected with death). Thus, violet is interposed to create a
triangular balance with white and green, the new Christian
colors, and signals the reawakening of conscience in every rite
designed as an act of penitence, forgiveness, and remission
of sins. The doctrine of original sin, its creation of evil, and
the Christian practice of contrition and absolution constitute
the other end of a constant polarity within the Catholic religion. This polarity was an aspect of Catholicism in which,
much later, in order to create a victorious image for itself
during the age of the Counter-Reformation, the confession,
direction and domination of the conscience would seem to
prevail over the original green and white rituals of baptism
and the Eucharist. In every instance, the Church's affirmation
of its political-secular power and of its hierarchical structure
will be expressed using the ancient-classical authority of

purple-red and the byssus white of princely dress, as in the sacrificial ritual of the Mass, where the red robe of Christ (*sagum*) and the martyrs is invoked. Red remains the color of the fiery sphere of Pentecostal faith that accompanies the white figure of the Trinity's third person, the fruit of love between Father and Son, a color of fervency that endows the dignity of bishops and the fullness of the Catholic priesthood (from Paul II onward). In this color, in the center of this circle of fire, one finds the *splendor* of the initiate's faith and his vestment, the reign of the Agnus Dei in the white robe of his earthly vicar.

Throughout all this, black, before becoming the distinctive color of the clergy and a symbol of a minister's faithfulness, remained a pagan symbol, not only of hell but of eternal damnation. Black, a negative, earthy color representing the condemnation of sin, was in opposition to the green fertility of Mass and the fruits of the church militant, a color unreconcilable with the celestial sphere, the homeland of the church triumphant. In contrast to the old distinctions made by the Romans, *caeruleus color*, blue, at one time the sign of a foreigner, became the sign of celestial confessionality and of the downfall of the reddish pagan deities.

The common use of "urban" terra-cotta red was the expression of the stability and productivity of potters, who enlivened their work through the use of sculpture, etching, and painting. Color was occasionally used for ceramic here and there; in particular, copper oxides were used to create gradations of green and iron oxides for yellow and yellow-green. In addition, color was used for certain elaborations in form that created the basis for a transformation of that reddish tint so identified with terra-cotta. The greatest variety of such effects using these materials mixed into earth or silicate mixtures would occur in the late Roman period in the form of the fantastic coloristic effects obtained in glassblowing. In fact, iron oxides, if suspended and blown into glass, assume not the reddish yellow color of terra-cotta but rather a green and blue coloration. The impossibility of purifying the silicate sand of any suspended iron particles is contained in the very word *vitrum*, which came to denote the bluish-green color of glass splinters and fragments. The purple-red color of gems could not yet be reproduced in glass, at least not until the most precious of all elements, gold, could be suspended in the substance, thereby obtaining a ruby red glass with the same brilliance and coloration of the gemstone.

These technical developments became used in progressively more arcane ways to symbolize the various Christian virtues, which could be embodied only by glasswork, mosaics, crystals and uncut gems, in their mixture of the divine with what was natural and human. The rarefaction and rapid transformation of classical colors under Christianity displays principles by which a new community was formed to integrate Latins and barbarians. Upon this new social foundation was built a new, more transparent form of color intended to unite all those baptized as Christians and made manifest by the translucence of water rather than fire. In the catacombs, away from pagan civilization and all its public idols, Christian colors—green, sky blue, white, and violet—were the filters through which liturgical values were secretly passed and by which a communal ecclesial identity was silently expressed. Moreover, the New Testament's plan for salvation became evident in the chromatic scheme it used, in comparison with the bichromaticism of white and red in the Old Testament. This contrast comes through best perhaps in the importance invested in sky blue, full of supernatural virtues, its materiality dissolved, a focus of contemplation, illumination, transparency. But not only blue: the traditional symbols of water, such as fish and fishing, appropriately reveal the continuity of the Christian mission in contrast with the momentary appearance of Pentecostal fire and of the white spirit that animates it.

Sky blue and green are united again in the interior design and the sacred glasswork of Byzantine and Romanesque mosaics, set in a background in which precious metals are dissolved in order to assert the luminosity of truth and in which royal purple becomes the exclusive attribute of the Christ in his dignity as pantocrator. In subsequent pictorial traditions, the Madonna came to be associated alternately with blue, as queen of heaven, and with red, as mother of God in an interchange that created the same effect. The new interior, evangelical colors were reflected in the preaching of Christ's gospel and in his promise of the kingdom of heaven, which could be seen only with the eyes of faith and reached only through grace. Christian color, as opposed to pagan color, becomes an image no longer in human form, something almost "identical in color," as Dante puts it so luminously (*Paradise* 12:11), which "changes as heaven changes" (A. Savinio).

In this regard, to sum up, Nietzsche's suggestions, amplified and confirmed by Oswald Spengler, on polytheistic colors (yellow and red) or monotheistic colors (blue and green) offer yet another ideological distinction: between the classical-pagan colors of "space" (yellow, red, and black) and the religious-sacramental colors of "destiny" (blue, green, and violet), with the double meaning of presence and absence. Rainbow-colored images and apparitions of fate, the unexpected revelations of oracular messages—these are no longer; they are replaced instead with will, spirit, and grace. The oracular wisdom of the classical world in this way is contrary to the "miracular" character of the Christian faith in salvation. The new color of Christian destiny becomes a principle that the ancient law of philosophical change (*panta rei*) must follow, because the life beyond, rather than life on earth, is eternal.

In light of the consideration and respect given by Christians to the color blue as a symbol of the promised kingdom and to green as a sign of the new community of believers, in the Muslim faith one sees, in turn, still within a monotheistic context, a reflected yet radical juxtaposition of the two colors: first, in green as the color of religion and the Prophet, then in blue or turquoise as a color of the new Islamic religion and community. There seems to be here an appropriation of the celestial sphere in order to clothe the earthly life of the mosques, houses, and cities, since the incompatibility of a color with a particular form or image renders it even more chromatically universal. We see this in, for example, the fragmentation of arabesques or the geometric designs of ceramics and mosaics, which reinforce the absence of sacred images in Islamic art, owing to the ban on image-making. Green, a sign of Islamicization, is not commonly used in Islamic art, but is reserved instead as a special sign of respect and veneration.

Other meditative colors, determined according to analogy with parts of the body and emotions of the soul, are used solely in religious practice or prayer. Here again, in the traditional red-black-yellow colors and dyes and in the spun woolen yarn of rugs built on a network of blue, the sacred intention of prayer rugs becomes manifest, in the "window" design, which opens upon images and tones of absolute green, opens onto the very colors of destiny that have been said to belong to monotheistic religions. By this differentiation, Islamic religion uses the sky blue color of the Judeo-Christian god, but inverts these values to represent in another fashion a theological-prophetic unity in which religion, culture, and politics tend to be one and the same thing. As with Christianity, the body of the church and the ministerial community adopted the ritual use of distinctive, clerical colors, which enforce a certain mode of behavior and come under the sacramental formula: black demands respect.[8] (The color system of the East is at this point continually confronted with Western culture. To give a general example, one sees how much the poem *The Seven Princesses* by Nezami (1141–1204) is a combination of a fantastic fable and celebrative epic narrative. Here, the seven colors "created by the influence of the seven planets" are authentic narrative structures, which establish the basic metaphors being used and allow them to flow within the fables, each of which is characterized by a different shade, which clothes the characters and typifies the setting.)

The sacred universe of green in the Islamic world, and in particular the pairing of green and turquoise, found a true match in its confrontation with the pairing of green and blue in the Crusades. Insignias, banners, and heraldic devices became recognizable signs of the Christians among the warring armies and were used, upon return to the homeland, to manifest one's service to the cause. Thus, the origin of heraldic colors, or *tinctures*, is to be found in the history of the Crusades.

The exact designation and assignment of these distinctive, personal tinctures—gules (bright red), azure (deep blue), sable (black), vert (green), purpure (violet), tanne (brown), aurora (orange), sanguine (blood red); along with the colors of precious metals, or (gold) and argent (silver), and the color of furs, ermine and vair—constitute the testimony, history, and tradition of their bearers and function to witness to the force and pageantry of war, with heraldic colors and various divisions acting as both decoration and symbols of victory. The banners of Western troops, shaped into various geometric forms with regular patterns of bands and stripes, are immediately recognizable designs, while the flame or sabre shapes of Islamic naval flags, finely stitched with patches of varied colors, create a color that is mixed and mimetic, rather than merely juxtaposed.

In the world of European chivalry, as with colors in Christianity, a contrasting pair of tinctures came into common use: blue and gold. These divine, precious colors came to be used to reinforce the power, dignity, and rank of whoever wore them, representing the solemn investiture of sovereignty from above, maintained and shown forth as privilege. With the bestowal of feudal titles following the Crusades, the Christian emperors' right to use gold and blue became more and more widespread, spilling over into the insignias of faithful paladins, members of the warrior nobility, as well as into the clothing and liveries of their servants and the standards of their households.

The extrinsic value of these colors came to be joined to their intrinsic qualities in the pictorial tradition of the Trecento. Greater attention to the grades and values of colors became an obvious part of painting technique with the use of pure gold leaf and blues of various price and quality. In contracts for paintings there often appeared a specification of tints in relationship to the various grades of devotion to be evoked by the images of the painting, in the following order: *latria* is the height of adoration, belonging to the Holy Trinity; *dulia* belongs to the saints, angels, and church fathers; *hyperdulia*, an intermediate level of adoration, belongs to the Mother of God. The wealth and costliness of the colors and the authenticity of their use constitute the basis for the value and appreciation of the painting. The contract between painter and patron was drawn up according to the amount of blue or gold expected to be provided or paid for, usually in relationship to the number of figures and the various ranks of their importance and placement in the painting, whereas the date of completion was left open to the discretion and will of the painter, with a modest contribution to living expenses during the actual period of work. The grinding, mixing, and fixing of colors always constituted the fundamental secrets of the various workshops until Cennino Cennini in 1437 was able to go beyond the limit imposed by guild traditions in order to liberate the painting profession. Cennini extolled the virtues of blue and gold, which were those of the profession as well: "Ultramarine blue is the most perfect, noble, and beautiful color, above all other colors, about which one can neither do nor say anything to add upon its perfection. . . . Of its excellence, I wish to speak at length and show you it as fully as I might. And listen well, so you may gain great honor and use. In this color, along with gold (which adorns all the works of our art), whether on walls or in paintings, everything is resplendent."[9]

At this point we have reached the new reign of rare and precious materials at which Marco Polo marveled in the kingdom of Badakshan: "Here there is a high mountain, out of which the best and finest blue is mined. There are veins in the earth of stones out of which this blue is made, and mountains whence silver is mined. And the plain is very cold."[10]

3

Colors and Form

THE APPEARANCE of azure blue in the heart of the Latin world, along with practical suggestions and rules for the manufacture or imitation of highly prized, noble materials, is documented in an important formulary, probably compiled at the time of Charlemagne, toward the end of the eighth century. The success of this newer, less centralized empire made artisans reorganize and codify the sum of their knowledge, a process made clear in *Capitulare de villis*, the fundamental legal code pertaining to the manufacturing complexes in which resident artisans worked. The treatise *Compositiones ad tingenda musiva, pelles et alia, ad deaurandum ferrum, ad mineralia, crysographiam, ad glutina quaedam conficienda, aliaque artium documenta* . . . brings together knowledge on the applied arts from diverse quarters— from Hellenistic, Byzantine, barbarian, and late Roman sources—but in such a way as to create a useful body of knowledge, entirely central Italian in character, that in some ways provided a basis for the efflorescence of art in Tuscany during the fourteenth and fifteenth centuries. The first edition of the manuscript, discovered in Lucca, was published through the efforts of Ludovico Antonio Muratori, within the Enlightenment climate of appreciation for all the applied arts.[1] The treatise might be compared with the *Papyrus leydensis*, traced back to Thebes and perhaps the oldest formulary of dyes and craft substances used at the time. This work, compiled around 400 C.E., seems to have arisen out of the cultural exchange between East and West that occurred in the Mediterranean between Rome and Constantinople; a copy reached Italy and began circulating in the sixth century, around the time of the Gothic-Byzantine wars of Belisarius. *Compositiones*, however, is the best summation of knowledge concerning the flowering of mosaic art in the architecture of the Ravenna of the Byzantine period, describing such things as the coloristic effects of oxides and metallic salts like copper-sulfate, cinnabar, litharge (lead oxide), and orpiment (arsenic trisulfide) on glass mixtures, techniques handed down directly from Greek and Roman manufacturing except for the appearance of *lazure*, of Indo-Arabian origin.

During the tenth and eleventh centuries, various collections of technical knowledge were first compiled in the form of manuals and recipe books, which would later appear in the fifteenth-century manuscripts that have come down to us. The *Liber de coloribus et artibus romanorum* and the *Mappae clavicula* bring together secrets dispersed throughout the heart of Western civilization. The former is signed as the work of Eraclius, probably an anagram or a pseudonym for a number of authors. Large sections of this treatise appear in subsequent manuscript manuals; its first modern (though incomplete) publication came in 1781, and a completely reedited version appeared in the following century.[2] The *Mappae*, on the other hand, is properly speaking a catalogue of recipes, with a very specific listing of elements and materials used for painting, and thus it represents the original fund of knowledge available to Italian painters, derived in part from the classical traditions of Theophrastus, Pliny, and Vitruvius.

In 1774 Gotthold Ephraim Lessing brought to light another treatise, the *Schedula diversarum artium* of Theophilus, a twelfth-century German Benedictine monk, thus signaling a rising interest in a theory of color that was to be developed further by Goethe and F. F. Runge. The *Schedula*, an encyclopedic, pictorial work, became a bible for the miniaturist tradition so influential in medieval German art; in it the listing of elements became even more exacting, didactic, and prescriptive in order to make uniform the work of these monks who collectively produced illuminated manuscripts. Similar texts, developed at the dawn of Europe's great period of painting, were not as much concerned with how to extract or grind different kinds of earth or essences, in the manner of Theophratus's botanical approach to color, as they were focused on sharing the secrets of fixatives and materials needed to obtain particular grades of dryness or hardness for use on various kinds of wood. Finely ground pigments were mixed with the yolk or albumen of eggs, with casein, or with lime, to create long-lasting tempera. Thus, despite the fleeting nature of its subject, the science of color became a single unified system thanks to the existence of enduring arts such as painting, glasswork, mosaics, ceramics, and enameling.

This compilation of color knowledge brought together the materials of dye work with experimentation on various fixatives sought after to supplant the unstable and impure substances still in use at the time. Substances like saliva, urine, earwax, and blood—responsible for the lowly status of the trades that used them—were gradually replaced with purer, longer-lasting, and less corruptible fixatives such as walnut oil, poppy seed oil, and linseed oil. Mixed with powdered pigments and essences, they were then applied to panels prepared from cypress, walnut, or spruce. These developments reached their peak in the fourteenth century with the publication of *Liber magistri Petri de sancto Audemaro de coloribus faciendis*. Its author, Petro de Saint-Omer, known as Fra Mauro, added to the information drawn from earlier treatises his knowledge of the green dyes of Rouen and Normandy. The red called *varantia* (from *garance* or *garanza*, madder) was used as a kind of tincture to determine the quality of the product, bringing forth denser, warmer colors like *chermes* (scarlet) or *crocus* (saffron). The treatise *De coloribus diversis modis tractatur*, composed under the pseudonym Alcherius in 1398 and 1411 and subtitled evocatively *Ad tingendam rosam*, may be compared to the other well-known treatise on manuscript miniatures, the fourteenth-century *De arte illuminandi*. This latter work, the complete and definitive text on the art of illumination, is itself an epitome of that art. For instance, not only does it describe minium, the red pigment derived from cinnabar, a mercurial mineral, but it also makes frequent use of it in the paintings. (Nowadays what is called minium or red lead is actually a saline oxide of lead mixed with linseed oil and used as an antioxidant varnish.)

These manuals on miniatures were virtual exercises in autobiography for the abbeys and convents that produced them. Along with the manuals we find, in the major Italian cities with a tradition of artisans and trading—Venice, Lucca, Florence, Pisa—charters, rolls, and registers of art that record the names of parties possessing the rights to the works or assets of a guild or, in certain cases, the names of agents in allied branches of guilds such as those for weaving or dyeing. The list of members of a particular artistic trade were preceded with a description of the nature of the goods produced along with any exclusive rights to certain types of work. Such records represent the result of the material knowledge that guaranteed the quality of and respect for the finished product, which was regulated according to strict standards. Both the head of the guild and its members were bound to guard the trade secrets that formed the underpinning of the city's economy and, through its products, its fame and fortune as well. In this way a conflictual knot in the production of crafts was tied, linking an artisan through loyalty to a particular product or workshop.

But the eventual fate of a "colored" object of artistic value, capable of embodying the history of an entire culture in itself, would break the code of silence. The "free" artist would be "liberated" from the bonds of guild masters and prices, creating an image of the artist as a manufacturer of forms who moves forward due to his talent and determination out of his original condition and away from the bonds of the guild. This movement makes clear the intention and predictions of Cennino Cennini, applicable to the fourteenth century and all of the fifteenth century. Cennini's well-known *Libro de l'arte* (1437) signals, more than any other contemporary formularies (for example, *Secreto per colori, Libro per colori*, and the *Manuale de Tatun*, written around the fifteenth century) the social transition from craftsman to artist. This transformation was made possible by a kind of Daedalean daring and ingenuity, which astutely combined the wisdom of experience with the long-held, valuable secrets of the older arts to create a new ability to appreciate nature through paintings no longer painted solely with colors once termed *naturales* but using an admixture of those termed *artificiales* as well. After all, the height of painting's artistry and achievement is in its color and has little to do with the calculation of the *praetium* (price), a point amply illustrated by the history of Italian art in the fifteenth century and by the history of color, which was the foundation for this tradition.

Other small treatises on dyes and colors that do not chronicle the great triumph of painting (from Cennino Cennini to Giorgio Vasari) were to become isolated from the main currents of thought of the era, such as the *Kunstbuch* of the Dominican monks at Nuremburg, a religious community itself rather isolated. In the context of the development of the guilds, the simple paintings contained in the *Kunstbuch* depict the "works of patience" in religious life and detail various operations such as cutting out the shapes of insects or plants and transferring these with coloration (cinnabar, indigo, orpiment) and other natural finishings onto cloth, operations used to create figurative effects quite similar to tapestry work, though obtained with techniques taken from printing or tie-dyeing. Because they take place at the very moment in which the great arts are born, such dyeing processes, despite their technical virtuosity, could be regarded as inferior, if one does not take into account how the results they obtain came back into vogue during the reemergence of craft techniques in the middle of the nineteenth century. These latter techniques produced objects prized for their rarity and workmanship, as opposed to those manufactured in mass by industry. Thus, the chintzes of the Liberty stores designed by William Morris, right down to the unusual and exclusive weaving by Mariano Fortuny, were produced using techniques not all that different from those described in an earlier time. It was in fact to the laborious and productive Middle Ages that the lonely aestheticism of the resurgent craft movement's cult followers looked, searching out the historical origins of those objects held so dear and in such affection, objects now useless from the perspective of the more worldly ambitions of the urban middle class of the late nineteenth century.

The medieval dye trade possessed a huge fund of botanical and technical knowledge, which highlighted the distinctive places of origin for any manufactured object. Tightly knit communities of resident artisans were in fierce competition with one another over the quality of goods, with results not even remotely comparable to subsequent market economies, since they did not possess the trade protections designed to ensure the prestige and value of dyes as part of the national economy (as during the reign of Louis XIV). For example, in certain regions of pre-Renaissance Italy, near the wool- and silk-dyeing centers of Florence, Venice, and Genoa, the ancient classical esteem for purple seems to have reemerged, so that if we examine the competition between pieces of dyed cloth in a list of nineteen colors, we could seven in shades between crimson (chermes), litmus, and "reddish purple," with a somewhat limited introduction of an oriental indigo (rather common despite the various forms and names given it: *baldacca, maccabeo, baccadeo* [from Baghdad]) distinct from ultramarine or lapis lazuli blue as well as from Prussian blue out of Germany. Here one sees the evocative confusion of origin with shade: the place (beyond the sea) becomes the color (ultramarine). In regions of France and in a more limited way Germany as well, the blue dye of woad emerged through the perfection of knowledge and practice, to be remembered in the fustian jackets (*pers*) of two small French cities near Paris: Provins and Chalons-sur-Marne, famous for this art. One thinks of this beautiful blue cloth trimmed in fur in connection with the finely clothed ladies in the *Très riches heures du Duc de Berry* as well as Jean Fouquet's portraits of ladies.

The green and black tones of Flanders are perhaps as famous and as common in figurative embroidery as the blue capes of Frisia. The two tones of black are distinguishable by the mode of their production: the warmer one, with hints of brown, is obtained through various baths in extracts of alder and oak (*jotta concina*), the other, with hints of blue like the plumage of crows, is created through lengthy soaking in woad. The triumph of black as the color of public clothing can be dated to the emergence of the pious middle classes of the Reformation and was enlivened only by the spray of a folded white collar. Thus we see in portraits by Frans Hals and Van Dyck these differing tones of black clothing, which reveal two different ways of life and thought among the same social class: the new, richer robes of a newer class coming into power (Hals) versus the sober black clothing representing older values (Van Dyck).

The effect of Inquisitorial black on society was brought into Italy by Tommaso Campanella ("black clothing suits our age") at the beginning of the seventeenth century and recalled in the "Fustian jackets" (*pers*): "Colors, enjoyed by every age and nation, reveal the habits of a people. And nowadays, everyone loves black: earthly, material, infernal, the color of mourning and sign of ignorance. The first color was sky blue . . . then red in its warlike cruelty; then vair and its seditiousness; then came white in the age of God Jesus, and all who were baptized wore white robes; and from then on, various colors until today we have come to black. Thus, we will return to white, according to the wheel of fate."[3] In some periods in the history of clothing, great stress is placed on black's uprightness, as one can see in portraits from the end of the seventeenth century and the first few decades of the eighteenth century, where black is used to create a sense of distance and respect. Even in cities noted for a mixture of social classes, such as Venice,[4] such clothing comes back to life suddenly around 1830, when, indirectly, military colors (red, blue, and white), begin to become practically a second suit of clothes, a "uniform" destiny for every citizen.

In the late Middle Ages, the sharing of secrets and the desire to possess the new techniques and new wealth connected to the privileges of the dye trade, which was protected by and associated with the city guilds, produced a migration of dye workers from one city and country to another (from Lucca to Venice and Genoa, but also from Brabant and Normandy to Florence). This social movement came to embody the desires and social aspirations of those workers who wished to throw off the heavy weight of servitude and taxation imposed on them by laws that made them dependent upon the trades of wool and silk weavers (as in Calimala, for example). Those laws ensured the inferiority of the dye guilds, whose work along increased the value of the cloth by anywhere from 20 to 30 percent. Thus, the conflict between the major arts and the minor or common arts finally died out when the dye guilds at last obtained autonomous status from the "wicked weavers" and began an internal process of differentiation and privilege, as with the *grand teint* and *petit teint* in France, the *Schoenfarber* (dye workers who used a variety of colors) and the *Schwarzfarber* (dye workers who used black). These latter slowly improved the quality of the goods through the use of various black dyes, having started with the unfortunate production of "gloomy, dingy" garments only to arrive at the acme of dye work, whereby they clothed nearly all the lower social classes of the late Middle Ages and thus, in this way, also colored the tattered rebellions to follow.

4

Color in Drawing and Painting

PERHAPS because of an increasing distance from the workshop formularies, the distinction between form and color in artistic production gathered support from classical philosophy and was broadened further by the neoplatonist theoretical developments of the Renaissance. The classical juxtaposition of drawing and color, in itself already a rather academic notion which was to become popular in the late Renaissance, seemed to gain credibility from a passage in *Poetics*[1] and not just from the perceptual relativism of Pseudo-Aristotle in a work on the substance of color published in 1497. This passage unmistakably accords the drawn form primacy over color, for the very same reason that in tragedy the *mythos*, being the totality of events, must be considered more important than "character," which is simply the element by which we judge the various motivations of the characters in the play. Similarly with colors: "one who haphazardly throws around even the most beautiful colors cannot delight the eye as one who has drawn a simple figure against a white background." This pronouncement by Aristotle seems even more frankly platonic than Plato himself, since Plato in the *Timaeus* regards colors with the same respect he gives simple geometric figures, which are beautiful in themselves, delightful playthings of the rational mind. Plato regards colors as matter's attempt to make itself into light—a notion especially dear to any idealist aesthetic—in the same way that thought surges forth out of "gradations of black."

Thus, at this point when perceptual psychology grows from the soil of Aristotelian relativism, the Platonizing categories of "fulgor" and "splendor" (brightness, brilliance) constitute, even in the thought of Marsilio Ficino, the basis for every principle of ideation. And at the same time among the naturalists of the Cinquecento the principle of "discolor" or "decolor" (colorlessness) bears only an apparent resemblance to that of *albedo* and *nigredo* (whiteness and blackness) and is actually closer to the notions of *calor* and *frigus* (heat and cold), principles of *generatio* and *corruptio* (generation and decay). According to Ficino, who was himself a sort of second, Arab-influenced Aristotle, water and air are white, fire is red, and earth is multicolored, leading to the creation of a catalogue and the delineation of a nomenclature that included even "incertes colores," those closest to light and darkness. In general, the predominance of form over color was maintained through principles of perceptual abstraction such as light and darkness (though not solely these) and functioned within the theory of painting to produce the uplifting, liberating effect that the plastic arts and painting particularly wished to create with their representations of reality. This predominance of form would remain an uncontroverted position in the arts, with color's obscenity and luminosity alternately attacked, until such a time as the true falsity of models came to be revealed, until form came to be regulated by pure colors, until the destruction of the frame itself, which had been the "form" of every painting and of every coloristic effect in the history of painting.

At the beginning of scholastic debates over the uncertain territory shared by Aristotle and Plato, Roger Bacon, who more than occasionally turned his attention to color, was able to pull together the various strands into a discussion that in itself altered the ethical *substantia* of color. For the monastic Bacon, light was a "celestial" product that nevertheless had to pass through matter and that, without losing any of its original ability to reveal red and yellow, was reflected in lucid, ethereal bodies and returned to its original state intact. These feebly materialistic notions, drawn by Bacon from Plotinus, served quite conveniently at the time to heal the doctrinal rift between Plato and Aristotle and restore a productive level of discussion, even with respect to Saint Augustine, who had called shadow "the queen of colors."

At the same time, however, medieval cities were using and producing color through a body of technical knowledge, with special attention given, as we have noted, to the production and display of blue and gold, colors that exalt the finest qualities of light and that are necessary to the laws of colors, despite Bacon's notions concerning the contaminating quality of matter. Such ideas would not prevail in the intellectual climate of the fifteenth century, when philosophical priority was given to form over color, for color cannot be traced to matter itself but exists only in its display and appearance.

Thus, a mechanism was described that in reality governs color, inscribing well-defined limits around it with something that precedes and substantiates its reality: the so-called *antigraphice* (an art that "goes before"), in other words, drawing.

Such ideas gained prominence at a time before the growth of a more critical and detached discipline, that of natural (optical) perspective versus artificial or artistic perspective. The former, natural perspective, influenced the arts by fixing the trajectories of visual lines to provide a frame within which the great variety of the world could be inscribed but that was always gracefully dependent upon colors, for if they were taken away, the perceiving, sensing subject would be without any substantiating principle whatsoever (in the opinion of Galileo). Without color, the perceived phenomenon would disappear and could not be examined independently from its fleeting appearance, revealing itself in this way to be an accessory, secondary. Even though by now it is a commonplace, the contrast between form and color, between the Florentine and Venetian schools of painting, is in reality a substantial difference, or at least it was when, at the end of the sixteenth century, astronomical observations made through telescopes led to very real doubts concerning whether these were real phenomena or merely apparent, artificial effects. Drawing in the fifteenth century, carried out along the scientific geometry of perspective, charged the figurative arts with the task of bringing forth wisdom and truth, while elsewhere the world of colors was still composed of a marriage of elements, seductive but merely apparent. Weren't all the arts simply an artificial world anyway? Wasn't painting the mere "ape of nature" (*simia naturae*) and all the plastic arts merely beguiling fantasies? This was still the subterranean disagreement, fortunately still unresolved, which continued alongside the historic sovereignty granted to the art of drawing in the face of discontinuous artistic production, as ever dependent upon security granted by law and tied to the uncertain fate of the individual artist's life and fortunes—just like color.

Long before artists' only concern with color become merely practical and individualistic, the medieval catalogue of colors became fixed into a rigid scale of values, against which Lorenzo Valla (1430) inveighed with humanistically informed intelligence. Valla pointed out the inadequacies of a color system based on social hierarchies, the result of colors' primary use in heraldry, which lent them their prestige. By differentiating themselves ideologically according to their specific, hierarchical nature, colors underscored differences, distinguished between classes, and represented dignitaries, a fact that gave rise to Valla's peremptory declaration concerning Bartolo di Sassoferrato's intrinsic stupidity and inadequacy: "stoldissimum esse aliquem de dignitate colorum legem introducere" (it is a very silly thing to introduce a law concerning the nobility of colors).[2]

The theoretical observations of Leon Battista Alberti, introduced in *De pictura* (1436) with regard to colors, also seem to reconstitute an elemental scale of materials, in itself quite close to Lucretius's treatise on the variety of colors and the colorlessness of matter on the most basic level of the atom.

Alberti writes as if philosophical thought on colors had as its sole object the definition of painting and its rules of representation: "I say indeed that a mixture of colors can give birth to an infinite number of other colors, but of true colors, like the elements, there are but four, from which all other colors are born. These are the color of fire, red; the color of air, blue; the color of water, green; and the color of earth, gray." This reassertion of an essentially classical (that is, Aristotelian) theoretical proposition acknowledges the objective necessity of the affirmation that primary colors become manifest according to the relative strength of light. This attitude is both "philosophical" and humanistic with respect to any practical uses to which colors were put, either commonly or in heraldry, and lent support to hierarchical orders through the greater or lesser value given to the objects they cover or to the subjects that require and clothe themselves in such colors. By holding this theoretical attitude, the artist impugns the nobility-based order of colors as the cause and effect of social conditions or status and attempts to provide something entirely different from the *praetium* of the color, its price, by substituting instead the value of his craft and his artistic production.

Leonardo da Vinci paid even more precise attention to the way in which color is perceived in the incomplete treatise *On Painting*, which can be considered the starting point for every subsequent examination of how a pictorial composition is produced with respect to light and shadow, especially for the laws concerning how these latter are perceived and contrasted with one another. At times, he considered seven colors primary, with the exception of black and white (blue, yellow, green, dark orange, tan-brown, violet, and red), at times just six (white, yellow, green, blue, red, and black).

Leonardo's propositions tend to supplement the linear perspective that rules drawing by furnishing a theory of colors and perception (aerial perspective) that balances the experience and conditions of perceiving both light and shadow. In this system of painting, the use of colors is governed by a "perspective of disappearance" wherein opacity or transparence take on value through the effect of the air's "thickness," as well as from surfaces that are more or less reflective. Dark shadows serve to highlight bright colors, and light reveals dark contours, but the same colors may be heightened by bright colors nearby or darkened by deeper ones. Thus, a "perspective of colors" not only introduces a theory of relativity into the perception of colors but perhaps provides the basis for a subjective theory of chromatic perception.

Alongside this perspective of colors, Leonardo's "aerial perspective" applies the principle of colored shadows according to whether an object is seen at a distance or nearby, immersed in the bluish thickness of the air, which underscores distance. The transparence and opacity of the air, bluer closer to the earth, thinner higher up, gives mountains a more intense coloration at the base and a rather weaker coloration toward the summit. The corporeality of things and the nature of the countryside seem to become detached more and more from bright colors as they move toward shadow, eventually losing even those colors from the play of the shadows themselves, such that colors may completely lose their luminosity and become shadows from the same distance, shadows that move toward light. For this reason, the classical notion of chromatic perception as strictly dependent upon the perception of rays of light filtered through a medium among a predetermined polarity of yellow (or red) as the color of light versus blue (or green) as the color of shadow becomes amplified by the "negativity" of shadow which, in Leonardo's thought, has a productive function. Thus he completely inverts the classical relationship between light and shadow: the perspective of disappearance and the aerial perspective determine the limits of vision, which become more and more rarefied and thus reveal the natural color of shadow. Leonardo invites the viewer to both an experiment and a game:

> If you wish to see briefly all the varieties of composite colors, take pieces of colored glass and look through them at all the colors of the countryside. There you will see that all the colors of objects seen through the glass blend with the color of the glass, and you will see which color is strengthened or impaired by such mixture. For example, if the glass is yellow, I say that the visual images of objects which pass through that color to the eye can be impaired as well as improved. Deterioration will take place with blue, black, and white more than with all the others, and improvement will occur with yellow and green more than with all the others. Thus with the eye you will consider color mixtures which are infinite in number, and in this way you will make a

choice of colors for innovations of mixed and composite colors. You will do the same with two glasses of different colors held before the eyes, and thus you will be able to continue by yourself.[3]

Here we see the reintroduction of a practice that will be proposed again by Delacroix (and even later by the Impressionists) concerning the blue or green color of shadow, evoking in the mixture of colors all those possibilities that emerge through the effect of "deprivation" or "subtraction," which would be deliberately created through painted impressions intuitively perceived as additive and productive:

The law of green for reflections and for the edge of shadow or for lengthened shadow, which I first discovered in the laundry, can be extended to everything, just as the three mixed colors can be found everywhere. I thought they were only in certain objects.

This is obvious at sea. The shadows thrown are obviously violet and the reflections are green, quite clearly.

Here we come upon the law that nature always behaves in this way. Just as a plane is composed of smaller planes, a wave of smaller waves, thus the light of day is modified and decomposes on all objects in the same manner. The most obvious law of decomposition is the one that first impressed me as an absolutely general principle, concerning the shininess of objects. It was upon certain objects that I was able to detect the present of the three shades of color brought together: a cuirass, a diamond, etc. One then comes across things, like fabrics, laundry, certain landscape effects, and, above all, the sea, where this effect is quite obvious. I did not delay in noticing that for flesh this effect is startling. Finally, I came to the conclusion that nothing exists that does not possess these three colors. In fact, when I come across laundry with a violet shadow and a green reflection, can I say that there are only two tones? Is not orange also necessarily present, since in green there is yellow and violet?[4]

Besides Leonardo's theoretical project concerning color, a sixteenth-century theory of colors begins with Antonio Tilesio in 1528 and in fact represents the conclusion of the Aristotelian philosophical tradition, which had at that time been reproposed on the basis of the rediscovery of the original text of *De coloribus*. This development, however, had been preceded by Mario Equicola in his *Libro de natura de amore* (Venice, 1525), which began a tradition of minor essays on love and on color with the purpose of "creating goodwill for ourselves," essays for the most part published in Venice, the renowned capital of color.

Antonio Tilesio's *De coloribus* went beyond the hierarchical tradition of the Middle Ages and had the intention of establishing, using hints gleaned from Aristotle, a principle of chromatic organization based on nomenclature, etymology, and the concordance of certain contemporary colors with those of the Greek and Latin classical world by way of their use and the written language that defined and controlled the substance of color. These "philological" colors made at least two Aristotelian writers, Giulio Cesare Scaligero and Simone Porzio (the latter having provided the translation and ample commentary on the Aristotelian-Theophrastean work on colors in 1548), institute the regulatory principle of primacy versus derivation of substances, which was based on the theoretical and historical teachings of specific texts. Tilesio provides a repertory of twelve colors for comparison, and his concordance of modern and ancient tones attests to the linguistic-generative trend of Renaissance thought concerning the body of Latin treatises on color. Thus, *caeruleus, caesius, ater, albus, pullus, ferrugineus, rufus, roseus, puniceus, fulvus,* and *viridis* constitute the map of the favorite colors of the Renaissance, which are then expanded into various families of colors derived from the respective dominant tones.[5] In the recorded list, the greatest difficulties in recreating the actual tone of the color were encountered with *rufus,* the reddish brown of rocks and hair; *fulvus,* the intense yellow color of grain and spun gold; and *pullus,* defined as a color of mixed, muddy gray such as found on the backs of hares, the Greek color of mourning, an "equal color" that imitates others and tends toward neutrality and obscurity.

Tilesio's work also has much in common with those treatises on color written with explicitly stated "romantic" purposes, which, for example, suggest ways of dressing that will send secret messages to the beloved through the wardrobe, ways of "talking" in secret through offering bouquets composed of flowers of certain colors. The first brief work of this kind, *Del significato de' colori* (The meaning of colors; Venice, 1535) by Fulvio Pellegrino Morato, brings forth several novel ideas that would be interesting to compare with contemporary paintings in which the artist speaks through colors rather than through composition. Others have suggested ideas along these lines, almost copying the concept, as in the *Dialogue in Which the Qualities, Diversity and Propriety of Colors Are Discussed* (Venice, 1557) by Ludovico Dolce and the *Most Monstrous Monster* (Venice, 1557) by Giovanni de Rinaldi of Ferrara, in which the intentions of readers to whom this work is directed are defined as follows: "for whomever with colors accompanied by art / would happiness or grief reveal to his beloved." Other Renaissance works on love and colors by Mario Equicola, Coronato Occolti, and Antonio Calli are to be placed squarely in the realm of sixteenth-century Italian literature on courtly behavior and are written in the idiom of Baldassare Castiglione's *Il cortegiano* (The Courtier) and Giovanni della Casa's book of etiquette *Il galateo*, which set the standards for this new culture, with signs and colors becoming new expressions of manners and fashions. Morato's short work served above all to highlight how the objective meanings of colors are actually insignificant if they cannot be bent to accommodate the technical considerations of suitability (*convenienza*) and appearance (*aderenza*), in order to avoid the sophistry of the "schools of learned philosophers [who] concluded that snow was not white but black." A sonnet usually precedes such interpretative exercises, introducing a language of individual colors as if providing a handbook of the joys and pains of life and human behavior: each of twelve lines describes a color, to which the final couplet adds the heraldic colors of silver and gold. Here green stands for hope, even if little is left; red for vengeance, cruelty, suffering; black for unhappiness over love and death; white for purity and truth, sincerity of heart and soul; yellow for control and arrogance; tan or dark orange (in Italian, *leonino*, the color of the lion's mane) for the intrepid soul, royal grandeur, and gratitude for gifts received; deep violet (in Italian, *morello*, the color of ripe blackberries) for love that destroys and scorn for life over that which is loved; green-gray for deceit; carmine for the pleasure of love; a mixture indicates eccentricity, fantasy, instability; light blue a high mind, magnanimity, sublime love; chartreuse desperation and the end of all hopes; silver suspicion and jealousy; gold everything rich and honorable.

The connections suggested by this system would become developed not according to the suitability of the color to whoever is wearing it but exclusively according to its appearance at that particular place and time, according to its effect on the eye. Thus, colors continue to become tonalities open to whatever suggestions might be made and by the chromatic sensibility of the Renaissance—distant from our point of view, to be sure, but which can be glimpsed in the sixteenth-century world of color customs, both in dress and in language. In this way *berrettino*, a color that "is and is not" between gray and ecru (as in raw silk), finds its companion in a tan-brown that is burnished gold, blond, or roan; chartreuse, the color of grass grazed upon by animals, is paired with flesh or red; light blue with yellow-orange (in Italian, *flameo*, the color of flame) and tan; deep violet (*morello*) with the green of leeks and the yellow of grasses; black with white and nothing else; white with pink or carmine. "Austere" colors are still deep violet or purple-blue. "Florid" colors are cinnabar, crimson, green (*chrysocol*), and indigo. "Sweet" colors are blond, beige, pink. Nature, rather than artifice, loves deep blue, green, brown-gray, and white. Deerskin and mouse fur (brownish grays) ambiguously complete the natural order of clothing. In fact, Morato thus underlines the indistinct halo of meaning that surrounds colors by expressly indicating their deceptive quality in the subtitle of his treatise: *Iris; or, A Daedalean Work Dedicated to the Contrary*.

Beyond pictorial-artistic or literary-courtly treatments, the magico-naturalistic treatises on color at the height of the sixteenth century (Paracelsus, Bernardino Telesio, Gerolamo Cardano, and Giambattista della Porta) could represent para-scientific deviations of another Renaissance going on at the time. Even if one turns away from a reexamination of medieval texts concerning "natural perspective," in reality the birth of science as a method of observation (optics) is still uncertain enough in its own principles to be unable to refrain from speaking of color.

White, black, and red, according to Paracelsus, are always mixed with the basic substance (sulfur) and evidence successive chromatic gradations derived from the elemental chemical reactions possible at any given moment. This idea is a branch of thought which will grow in a rather overpowering way, incorporating the whole alchemical body of work on the production of colors, beyond those termed "apparent" (physical) or "imaginary" (psychological). Bernardino Telesio in *De colorum generatione* (1570), writing against Aristotle's abstract taxonomy, downplays the generative principles that had by that time entered into the Aristotelian nomenclature of the early sixteenth century through his analytic maxim "iuxta principia naturae" (close to the natural principles of matter that compose them); he considers *calor* and *frigor* as basic aspects of *generatio* and *corruptio*, dialectical categories that introduced doubt into the foundation of certainties built by classical authorities. Furthermore, these categories introduced a criterion of observation based on similarity and difference in its conclusion that everything material behaves according to the laws of matter ("from matter to materials"). The evidence derived from "physiological" colors in reconnecting the material effect of color with its material causes can be seen even in the Theophrastean methods of "physiognomy" or characterological morphology espoused by such authors as Polemone, Adamantius, and della Porta. This connecting of color and character can be seen, for example, in the comparison of "complexions" and "temperaments" as signs of characters reflected in the face and body (phlegmatics, cholerics, sanguines, melancholics, or necrophytes; clear-tempered, reproductive, aggressive, adipose). As types and as human behaviors, these are simply new categories with respect to scholastic nominalism. However, there have already emerged at this time powerful new techniques of combination and differentiation. These techniques, present even in the platonic order of the *humana fabrica* as the subject for the *harmonia mundi*, may not have immediately resulted in the aggregative structures necessary for knowledge, but eventually they emerged through patient observation and interpretation. This naturalistic and physiological technology, which brings the artificial into relationship with the natural, can be seen indirectly as a kind of anatomical science, creating a subject little by little so as to gain knowledge of vital functions, a kind of interpretive, simulative art that knows the object of observation by entering into it, a natural pairing of method and knowledge. Similarly, within this protoexperimental body of knowledge, Gerolamo Cardano makes distinctions between principal colors and observations in a still vaguely Aristotelian way. He uses a method of individuation with classical nomenclature that was recast "according to the principal differences between colors," on the basis not only of the recent Telesian distinction between *humiditas* and *siccitas* but also with reference to the nature of crystals and precious gems as a means of color perception. Here as well he introduced certain concepts, by no means primitive, concerning reflection, refraction, and the effects of chromatic privation or production on rays of light. In this new process of color analysis there now existed the distinction between color material that is objective or alchemically producible and a chromatic *substantia* mediated by sensory perception as schema of rational form of sight. The phenomenon, in reality, is grasped through its appearance: just as the space that lies between is the means through which light passes, so too is the physiological nature of the eye that observes while being observed itself.

*   *   *

Yet from Giotto di Bondone up through the Renaissance, the history of artistic excellence would be one of the individuality and inspiration of pictorial invention. The golden-azure world of colors would be based more and more on the distinction between drawing and form, as these detach themselves more and more from the body of their effects and become rarefied transfigurations or plans which by themselves cannot serve as representation. The secret power of color is thus held back and continues to develop through the art of combinations, additive or subtractive, as in the arcane "art of memory" from Raymond Lull up to the wizard Giulio Camillo Delminio. Far from any theoretical simplification, it was the notable possession of those whose brilliant secret was revealed only through reflections of hidden powers. From such a situation emerged the historic primacy of the Florentine artists who were, above all, artists of design, while the Venetians would be considered painters who merely trafficked, like merchants, in the economic play of artistic value and the sale of goods, known for the dazzling tricks played on various individual objects and for the entrancing advertisement of their world of business.

The idea expressed by Paolo Pino in *Dialogo di pittura* (Dialogue on painting, 1548)[6] of profiting by combining the virtues of Tuscan design with those of Venetian color is a literary proposal of truce far from the spirit animating artistic production at that time, as is clear in the *Aretino* (1557)[7] of Ludovico Dolce, a proponent of a courtly Renaissance use of color. The spirit of the time was rather more full of effects, but not simply due to an affection for symbolism. This is seen in the political artistry of Titian, who struck a stable agreement between artist and ruler with an exchange of diplomatic acts: the artist paints a portrait of the monarch, the monarch bows to receive the fallen brush of the artist. This situation would seem to clearly designate the artist as a kind of demigod in the world of images, in the perpetuation of the history of dominion that, more than historical writings, is the most enduring effect of glorious political or military actions. The apprenticeship of theory to practice would become more and more detached from imitation and the reproduction of models, which had been the most effective response of artists under the yoke of slavery to the power of the Church and artistic patrons. In contrast to this, the *libertas* of design comes more and more under the obligation of the presumed *obseqium* of color, which lends its tribute through a relevation of form that has been rendered a pure effect of its appearance.

The reds that appear in works by Giorgione (which to Giorgio Vasari's eyes "falsifies the freshness of living flesh"),[8] Tintoretto, and Titian are not simply a pictorial invention but are the result of practice involving cosmetics (rouge based on kermes, "dragon's blood," and brazilwood, made by women at home). The red appearing in Titian and Palma Il Vecchio is mostly a hair dye that produces a bright blond color and was used in outdoor displays and in the scenery produced for festivals, regattas, and carnivals, the so-called people's theater. *L'espoitrinement à la façon de Venise*, or Venetian-style exhibitionism, was for the traveler and old-time tourist, as one can imagine, above all manifested in the colors of that illusory city.

The festival of both permanent and temporary color artistry that followed the triumph of painting was marked more profoundly by the deep red of weeping wounds, blood drawn in the naval battles of the fifteenth and sixteenth centuries, where the blood-stained banners and equipment of the old sword-carrying armies crossed paths with the gun-carrying armies of a newer era. The material process of aging made a painting, like a body, prey to an interior process of corruption and could thus confine Rembrandt's brown to the realm of "Protestant" colors (Spengler) in contrast to Grunewald's Catholic green. The materials of painting were by now revealed as leftovers from an organic life that had ceased to pulsate, above and beyond the price and respect earned by the thriving Protestant traders, with their sovereign indifference to all such things. The color of daylight, which comes into a space and surrounds a Flemish portrait "in black," is now a gold coin, the ring of money in those clear, eager eyes. Rembrandt, however, showed that, through a mixture of inward, contrasting materials, this honorable material of wealth, which had become the earnest desire of this "golden century," could be transformed into a joke, into a dung heap. When he says that those with delicate noses should keep their distance from his paintings, Rembrandt affirmed that the artist can pull off the diabolic joke of exchanging, at whim, the most precious goods with the poorest and most vile. The tragedy of matter-color is recited yet again by Delacroix, who would have liked to create, in the manner of a latter-day demiurge, flesh out of mud. This divine and diabolical joke, this *merde d'artiste*, carries with it a sign of punishment and condemnation, the expulsion from paradise and the Promethean punishment meted out to whoever uses horrible artifice to transform colored material into nothing but excrement.

Venetian color, insofar as it is linked to the artistry of an entire city, has within itself the human qualities of color (those of feces and of blood), thereby succeeding between the sixteenth and seventeenth centuries in bringing together different areas of pictorial production and culture, those of Northern Europe with those of the Latin countries. Venice as capital of color and painting made use, particularly in the production and distribution of goods, of that specific increase in manufactured value obtained through the use and communication of secrets drawn from the dye trade, the sweat of the dyer's brow. One work is notable in this regard as the veritable bible of color with respect to the means of color production in the sixteenth century: *Plictho de l'arte de tentori* (Notebook on the dyer's art, 1548) by Giovanventura Rosetti, with its universe of producible dyes, along with *Secrets of the Perfumer's Art* (1555), with its world of perfumes and scents, placing both colors and scents into a laboratory of essences, a crucible of inspired sensations.

Beyond this, once the Roman Academy of Design, spurred on by Federico Zuccari, chose drawing by imitation and mannerism as the necessary apprenticeship for pictorial training, adopting the style of various arts and trades in order to direct and regulate the quality of production and to assure uniformity between the fine and decorative arts, color remained emblematically the delimitation of a dark border, illuminated by the light of a candle, beyond which lay anarchy and the rupture of the art of painting. In light of such a situation, it is interesting how Giovan Paolo Lomazzo, who sketches out a similar movement and interruption in his *Treatise on the Art of Painting, Sculpture, and Architecture* (1584), deals with the fate of colors by uniting them with astrological insights and with the hard fate suffered by divinatory, "judicial" astronomy under the sanctions of the Counter-Reformation. In this way, he anticipated the completely psychological effect colors would have beyond the well-tended garden of painting, not too unlike the excursuses on the meaning and courtly significance of colors by such authors as Equicola, Morato, Dolce, Rinaldi, Coronato Occolti, Andrea Alciati, and Antonio Calli. In tracing a line of demarcation between literary and alchemical uses of the discourse and appearance of color, Lomazzo also includes the material knowledge of such protoscientists as Cardano and della Porta and uses it to establish, in his *Ideas on the Temple of Painting*, a linear scheme crossed at various points by values present in the "natural magic" of della Porta (magico-astrological signs corresponding to actual categories of perception): proportion, movement, form, light, composition, perspective, and color. In the classificatory model of artists, these values become the "champions," the "seven rulers of painting." To be sure, the body of Michelangelo Car-

avaggio's work, along with that of his many followers, seems
to deny any knowledge of academic drawing as a formula and
ethical basis of the arts, even if it is not actually true (as shown
by recent X-ray photographs of his paintings) that he did not
draw at all before painting. For him, the drawing has become
disseminated under and into the skin of the painting, like a
tattoo. Thus, it is not entirely strange for Roger de Piles in
"Scale of Painters" at the end of his *Cours de peinture par
principes* (1708) to consider Caravaggio's reversal of traditional
values as a result of his use of color, the effects of which "are
as alluring to the eye as the loveliness of verse in poetry"
(Poussin).

According to de Piles, the acme of color is reached by Giorgione and Titian, while Raphael receives the highest average
score across all four categories of painting values (composition, drawing, color and expression), followed by Rubens,
whom de Piles contrasted with Poussin, an artist whose use of
yellows and blues, though beloved by the neoclassical devo-
tees of pure drawing, is quite at odds with the basic colors of
flesh and gold used by Rubens and Rembrandt.[9] But Caravaggio's colors still remain dim in the eyes of his later critics,
contrasted not with drawing but rather with expression, and
this category of expression, in which the more brilliant notion
of "invention" seems to hide, lies less in the "character of the
object than with the thoughts of the human soul." One cannot deny that certain components of Caravaggio's drawing
have "taste and precision," but it is the "negativity" manifested in his works that one perceives about all, his negativity

concerning a plunge into rationality, into a "preestablished harmony" of the universe, which one must be "enlightened," rather than desperate, to believe.

This color, so full of shadow and impurity, does not disturb the inductive method used by Francis Bacon in his *Sermones fideles, ethici, politici, oeconomici* (1644), in which colors are simply characters, signs, aspects, indications of difference, rather than positive images; nor dies this sort of color trouble Galileo (1623), for whom colors, like odors and tastes, become mixed according to the variability of who is perceiving them and can only reveal themselves to be "secondary" phenomena of scientific interest with respect to those considered "objective," such as form, movement, and numbers.

> Still I say I feel myself pulled by necessity, as soon as I perceive a corporeal substance or material, to conceive of how it is delineated or configured by this figure or that, how it stands in relation to others larger or smaller, whether it is in this place or that, this time or that, whether it moves or is still, whether it touches another object or not, whether it is one, many, or few, nor can I in my wildest dreams imagine thinking of it outside these conditions; however, whether it is white or red, bitter or sweet, loud or soft, aromatic or offensive to the nose, I do not feel my mind compelled to apprehend such conditions with relation to it: indeed, if our senses had not been given to us, perhaps discourse and imagination itself might never have occurred at all. What I think of these tastes, odors, colors, etc., as a part of the object which it seems to us to possess, these are but

mere names, which reside only in a sensitive body, so
that were the animal in us removed, so would these
qualities be removed and canceled out; and yet, having
imposed upon these things particular names different
from those of the other true, first qualities of existence,
we would like to believe that they are in fact really and
truly different.[10]

These considerations were taken up again quite amply by
John Locke in his *Essay Concerning Human Understanding*
(1690). At the end of the sixteenth century, as we can see in
the various works on optics by Maurolico, Mirami, Galileo,
Kepler, Descartes, Scheiner, and Aguillon, the sight and perception of colors becomes gradually separated from a science
of observation, a new approach developed partly as theory
concerning sight, partly as the physiology and mechanics of
the eye-as-machine and ocular aids such as the telescope or
microscope: objects that by receiving rays of light produce
absolute confirmation of all the nocturnal observations of the
new astrologers.

Against this obliteration of chromatic perception down to a
white monochromatism of pure vision, a chapter entitled
"Chromocritica" by the Jesuit Athanasius Kircher in his *Ars
magna lucis et umbrae* (1646) presents the world of color as
irrevocably tied to the realm of shadow. This position will
remain the standard throughout the entire Catholic encyclopedic enterprise of the mid-1600s, from Lazzaro Nuguet to
Caspar Schott, peers of Kircher, along with analogous observations by the Venetian bishop Marco Antonio de Dominis,

who in 1611 proposed that color is born from an equal mixture of darkness and light. In this way, the action of light "deprivation" works directly on material bodies to induce chromatic tonalities that are more or less freed from the encircling world of aerial space and thus are able to generate, as Leonardo asserted, a dominant color out of shadow, which functions as "the subtle form of light."

There is no doubt that the vast encyclopedic enterprise of the Jesuits in the seventeenth century was meant to encourage the development of all those *artes secundariae* that had been so quickly claimed by Galileo and Descartes and, along with these (supposedly) the science of colors as well, as a way of bringing their power to bear on the eyes of conscience. Kircher's *ars magna* and Schott's *magia universalis* soon became bound into a tight framework of intellectual aspiration. Their work was spurred on by an eagerness to sound out the depth and extent of every unknown scientific field, spurred on by an ideological desire to reestablish the dominion of knowledge over a power growing steadily stronger and more widespread, not unlike the power of sin on the conscience or of death on the body. The *ars moriendi* of the seventeenth century thus is the ripened fruit of this production cycle of knowledge and desire. The *magna arte* that relieves confusion and fear seemed to draw its strength—and here is hidden the diabolical intelligence of this program—from renunciation of what can be best and most bountifully obtained without the use of experimental science or mechanics. As the manuals of *ars moriendi* instruct, intellectual life should consist of training the individual no longer to desire a life of the mind, in favor of a tangled system of practices and spiritual exercises meant to aid the devotee to pass his life in a mixture of rapturous delight and suffering (the *eupatia* of St. Francis of Sales). Thus the *magne arti* of the Catholic encyclopedias appear to renounce truth and scientific evidence but in reality reveal rather well the actual mechanics of complex and uncategorizable phenomena that lay science did not concern itself with, such as physiology, etymological linguistics, and archeology. Generally speaking, however, the jesuitic question actually raises another, more relevant point: of what interest is empirical truth if the spread of science (or scientific knowledge) is based on consensus and the establishment of consensus?

All of this corresponds to themes articulated by Kircher in his work on "light as shadow," a work composed of various parts: *catoptrica* (mirrors), *parastatica* or *diottrica* (lenses), *gnomonica* (meridians and solar timepieces) and a compendious *sciografia* (theory of shadow). The latter was already included in *Books on Perspective* by Guidobaldo del Monte and in *Curious Perspective* by Jean-François Niceron. Kircher's work gives a different answer from those texts on the archeological matrix of a world where colors are seen as "children of shadow." Shadow in fact—according to Kircher's propositions—is the portrait of a man's life rendered with almost religious attention to detail, since man is "always and everywhere unexpectedly faced with his own death." In such a sublime sight the soul of triumphant Baroque, which Athanasius Kircher had a hand in creating, begins to articulate a program of religious technology similar to the fervent laicism of the Enlightenment.

"All that is visible in this world is so through light mixed with shadow, through a sort of clarified darkness. Colors are therefore the properties of an object obscured, of a darkened light. . . . The world can no longer be called the cosmos."[11] These words, which Goethe would make his own in establishing a new surge of interest in color (unlike Newton), reenter the discussion on the discovery and use of an apparatus similar to the eye and to light, at first without reference to the specific subject of colors and yet indispensable to their observation and recognition: namely, the camera obscura. Here both science and pre-Newtonian magic, which had remained devoted to color, find themselves not too far away from artistic experience along the "shadow line" where colors are defined and identified as "true, apparent, and intentional." Moreover, at the height of the seventeenth century, the use of filtering apparatuses would render the uncertain certain by producing the first evidence that light destroys color while shadow produces it, thus giving rise to an analogy to Catholic confession, which requires contrition and fear of guilt, rather than consciousness, to produce the positive action of forgiveness and grace. For this reason, gravity, prudence, and consensus need to be reread in the key of color as truth, appearance, and intentionality. Awareness of this profound negativity with respect to the universe creates, in the eye and the body, an exaltatory practice of confession (*motus conscientiae*) and the gratifying ability to receive or grant forgiveness in a soul that would otherwise be damned by terror and the shadow of sin. Father Kircher exhibits his "diabolic" machine as the wooden, filtering box of the confessional: the magic lantern he employs in his sermons is none other than the inverted principle of the camera obscura, intended to highlight the terrifying images of death, eternal hell fire, and damned souls to create the true internal "apparitions" that, in the sonorous words of Baroque preaching, can exist without body.

In any case, in the seventeenth century a clear distinction is made: art and magic fight for the idea of a shadow-line concept of colors as opposed to experimental science, which considers chromatic phenomena a rather unexplainable, secondary effect of observation and optical perception. From this struggle is born the scientific success of Newton's experiments, which, in introducing and resolving the phenomenon of color perception, the weakest and most ignored point of Cartesian science, becomes in fact the proving ground of his entire system of thought. The heretofore vague subject of colors thus suddenly is restored to the phenomenon of light and is made part of a theory whose brilliance will clarify in a marvelous way everything else in Newton's scientific thought, serving to shore up the more fragile and theoretically modest system of ideas concerning his own practice as a scientist. The frankly instrumental investigations of Newton's work on optics (here we must note how Robert Hooke's work in the same area was contemporaneously obscured) used the spectacle of colors to legitimate the whole of his scientific theory, its use and diffusion as well as its methods. In sub-stance, it was the most successful example of the *onus probandi* of the new science and of the unstoppable momentum in the history of humankind, which, from that moment on, changed its collective mind on the laws of gravity and the acceleration of falling bodies by virtue of the stupefying events in the spectrum of colors.

5

Color and Its Order

THE ARTIFICIAL PURITY of Sir Isaac Newton's experiments
with light, conducted after 1666 and reported in *Lectiones op-
ticae*, perfected techniques of astronomical observation by way
of the catoptric telescope, which inverted the traditional
model of Galileo's looking glass. This, conversely, provided
him with the necessary evidence to support the challenge he
had launched in his conclusive report on his experiments with
light, *Optiks* (1704). The principal object of this work was
precisely to assert that the refraction of a ray of light into the
colors of the chromatic spectrum was a "necessary" phenomenon. Newton's hypothesis, which drew forth an avalanche
of observations and protests, cost him, in his own words, "for
a mere shadow, the loss of sleep, and yet an important and
substantial good." We have seen how the two major sides in
the discussion of colors distinguished between light and
shadow, objects more or less physical, more or less material.
A third side—or, more accurately, a third component of the
discussion—examined both the conditions of passage from
one to the other and the media through which light passed,
giving rise to shadow but without negating the chromatic
materiality of the objects perceived. Robert Boyle, who was
extremely close to Newton and in some ways anticipated him,

posed the problem of the mechanical modification of light rays reflected or refracted by the molecules of a transparent body. Francesco Maria Grimaldi (1665), more accurately but with all the uncertainty and relativism typical of the Galilean age, was the first to consider the phenomenon of light an imponderable element composed of innumerable transparent molecules, which could be subjugated and slowed to a frequency and a wavelength: colors, thus, were the products of reflection and refraction and were themselves light made perceptible to our vision under certain conditions. These chromatic observations still pertain to light as *object*, while Newton instead seemed inclined more toward points of view that fell somewhere between light and shadow. One such view was that of Marco Antonio de Dominis, who announced, in the name of light, that the observable material world was in reality completely dark. The faithful, however, were not disposed to renounce thinking of the universe as created in color nor to accept a mournful universe consigned to eternal grayness, illuminated solely by the deceptions of chromatic appearance.

And yet darkness was all around, and gradual enlightenment came by way of Newton's empirical findings, brought forth by experimental methods so simple that the result was a kind of absolute research, contributing greatly to the elegance of his scientific theories. The most attractive effect of Newton's optics could be found in the fact that the refraction of a ray of light produced not only decomposition into the spectrum of colors but the possibility of reconstituting the totality as well by inverting the process and producing white light once again. This, not uncoincidentally, was called the crucial experiment (*experimentum crucis*), since separating rays of light remained the simplest and most singular experiment, in an absolute sense, on a phenomenon at that time still as obscure as the perception of light and the physiology of color perception. The play of the intersecting prisms presented completeness and truth, experimentally both necessary and sufficient, and explained by means of a well-founded theory a phenomenon that could be observed and reproduced by any educated person, even nonspecialists. This phenomenon could be seen by whoever could make use of his own intelligence to think with the same clarity on the cultural, "enlightening" message provided therein to clarify the shadows of falsehood and prejudice. Never had such a simple phenomenon been considered so vast and rich with truth.

Indeed, seized by Italian and French intellectuals such as Voltaire and Francesco Algarotti, it was made the entire program of Enlightenment ideals.[1] Newton's experiments therefore appeared especially brilliant, even if rotating his wheel, divided into sections of seven colors, the mystical number of English magic, regaled the eye

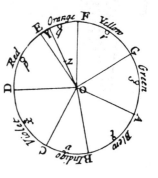

FIGURE I

92

with an indistinct grayish image, like Tycho Brahe's future-telling crystals. This image was said to be in fact white, its apparent grayness due to the imperfection of our perceptual instruments. Newton's wheel (see figure 1) astonishingly summed up the entire phenomenon into a theory so perfect that it was virtually inapplicable to the vastness of the phenomenal world, much in the same way as Boyle's molecular laws on gas, to which Mariotte (1688) added certain orthopedic prostheses, castigating the theory while at the same time enabling it to move forward.

Although the faithful scientific campaign on behalf of Newton waged by John Desaguliers had ended the famous eighteenth-century quarrel on the laws of "motion and color," opposition arose in the figure of Giovanni Rizzetti, who wondered pointedly why the entire world and all the various objects clarified by Newton's colors did not appear to be painted by the polychrome stripes of the Newtonian rainbow. This same author in *De luminis affectionibus* (1721) posed the first psychological objections, by distinguishing between the chromatic sensations of "natural, apparent, and imaginary" colors, distinctions already promulgated in the encyclopedias of the Jesuits (true, apparent, and intentional colors) and taken up again by Goethe in his explicitly Rizzettian exposition of the subject (chemical, physical, and physiological colors).

Newton's opponents turned toward a model of scientific explanation in which a few clear arguments were brought together in an exemplary way to explain the whole complex phenomenon of light and color, connecting quite elegantly the seven fundamental colors to intervals of sound. Apart from objections concerning the problem of the seven fundamental colors—which was itself questioned in *Notions élémentaires d'optique* (1784) by Jean-Paul Marat, who before the revolution was hardly a dilettante on the problem of color—every other objection was based on the divisibility and dissolvability of the *summa* of Newton's experiments. For example, one objection was based on distinguishing dispersion from refraction, which, according to Newton, followed well-known relationships of proportionality. It was demonstrated that refraction can occur without the appearance of the chromatic spectrum. Hence the terms "dispersion" and "dispersible" for the appearance of the chromatic spectrum were definitively substituted for "refraction" and "refractible." The latter terms are not necessarily tied to the emission of colors, but are perhaps mostly connected to "geometricism" of light, as expounded in Descarte's *Dioptrics* and *Catoptrics*. The well-founded arguments of Newton's opponents mitigated the definitive and perhaps metaphysical impact of Newton's *Optics* and the supraordinate *experimentum crucis*. Thus, colors, through a practical ordering system that still conventionally adhered to the notion of the seven Newtonian colors, were soon reduced to the mere three (red, green, and violet) of Thomas Young, similar to those propounded by the "color-blind" Senophanes of Colophon (purple, red, and yellow-green). This reduction followed on the heels of an interest in the measuring of chromatic tonalities present in so-called additive phenomena, and in the end, colors were reduced further to two once the phenomena of diffraction and refrangibility had been established by John Dollond. The old "ideological" colors of light and shadow appeared once more in the blue and yellow of Marat and eventually Goethe, two distinctly anti-Newtonian colors. The result here was that a latent chromatic mysticism came to be introduced and stood in opposition to the scientific pretensions of essential truth.

If it appeared that the chromatic wheel had been halted by a reaffirmation of classical dualism equidistant from light and darkness, a vigorous and productive push forward in colors was born. Friedrich Hegel in *Esthetics* (1817–29) discerns in the historical discourse on colors—that is, in the search for a harmony as "figure"—the dialectical synthesis that, in the world of colors, seemed both obvious and natural: that synthesis "resides in the subtraction of their crude difference and opposition, which, as such, is canceled out in a way that shows in their very differences their agreement with each other. In fact, they belong to each other reciprocally, although color is not unilateral but is an essential totality in itself."[2] Even in the arts a comparison began to be made between the harmony of colors and the harmony of sounds, in the relationship between colors and the half tones of the chromatic scale, tying together in one fell swoop the differentiation of the German *Bildung* between the successive arts (those of time) and the simultaneous arts (those of space). The concept that *timbre* was basically the aspect that defines the diversity of colors came into currency, while *tone* was held to be a principle of uniformity and mixture. In fact, the timbric color of impressionist art was juxtaposed to the avant-garde's tonal painting built up by contrasting effects (a technique that in music was called *Klangnmelodie*, exemplified in the "yellow sound" of Wassily Kandinsky (1912). In this context, the highly chromatic expressionism of Arnold Schoenberg or Aleksandr Scriabin seemed to retrieve historically the "deformations" of an artist like Giuseppi Arcimboldo, who had manufactured a "clavichord of colors" no less strange than Scriabin's *clavier à lumière*. Rudolph Steiner's *The Essence of Colors* (1914–24) and his art of eurhythmics were a resummation of this notion of "color-image" (red in the past, blue in the future) and of the "color splendor" of the protoromantic mysticism of Philipp Otto Runge. Runge was the writer whose artistic production was almost obsessively compressed into his *Farben-Kugel* (1810), a true Valhalla, the "ultimate art" as described in Goethe's *Farbenlehre* (1808–10).

Leonhard Euler's definition, with the refinement of sublime or infinitesimal calculations, seemed to distance itself from the ancient world of colors, here coldly described as "a series of isochronal vibrations," a notion that exists even today in the variation that "color is an emission of energy within well-defined frequencies," the last word in the physical history of colors. Such notions are centered on the nexus of matter-energy-color, even in relation to the cosmological creation of color and to the life of the stars, which flare up in blue and die in red. These ideas are a means of theorizing about colors that verges on not speaking about colors at all, isolating through a system of measurement the visible traces of what is perceived, which becomes, from now on, the object of various systems of classification.

Newton's laws and subsequent scientific accommodations served to introduce into a phenomenon as widely debated as the dispersion of light a principle of greater certainty, supplied by the development of the new sciences, which made possible reduction and analysis of a phenomenon as inconstant as the emission of light, and did so with the simplest instrument in the world: a glass prism. In this way, color theory would no longer be the exclusive domain of painting; science would take it away, just as the optical camera would steal the most well-worked secrets of pictorial representation.

Colors would no longer be a mode of pictoral production, but the transmission of light. Techniques of measuring and grading colors with respect to the intensity of emission of an illuminated object would stand in direct relation to well-defined color. For this reason, in the eighteenth century, the century of metrology and models, the first examples of colorimetry were built. Johann Heinrich Lambert's pyramid (1722) takes up the elementary trichromatic base, later to be propounded by Jakob Christoph Le Blon (1735). The pyramid was a geometric figure resembling a prism with a clear apex and a violet base and whose face displayed the various colors according to the order of their tonal emission (red, orange, yellow-green, indigo, violet). Johann Tobias Mayer (1745) had previously developed a principle of chromatic inversion illuminated by two triangular pyramids attached at their bases, in which color begins at the light upper vertex (brilliance) and ends in the dark lower vertex (saturation). This, then, is the basic concept behind which all successive colorimetric models would be aligned, from Runge's "mystical sphere" to the collection of color samples in skein form proposed by Albert Munsell (1905), to Wilhelm Ostwald's double cone (1915) and Harald Küppers's sparkling rhombohedron (1958), which combined them all. Küppers's colorimetric work remains a point of reference by virtue of its completeness.[3]

Newton's experiments on the dispersion of light, by opening the way to measurements and to the conventional color card, thus brought to a close the productive history of color as a function of light and shadow. Those experiments had pushed toward a final determination of the fundamental colors and their complements, no longer according to the archaic presence or absence of the qualitative world of colors, but rather in relation to the possibility of experiencing an impression of light and of reproducing that impression by way of predetermined effects. In this sense, the revelation of light as continuous and producible confirms not a fortuitous chromaticity and its secondary effects but rather the primacy of the source with respect to a constant emission. This source, measured with models and scales, can determine brightness, tonalities, and darkness. Color and light are reduced to data—as easily and conventionally understood physico-mathematically as the number zero. This sovereign interest in the source of light creates a distinct lack of attention to light's "negative or absent" forms (Leonardo's "disappearances," for example), the loss of intensity in relation to the means through which light passes; as such, it is an attitude entirely consonant with the scientific-ideological optimism of the Enlightenment: hypotheses (particle and wave) ignore the ancient ways of colors, casting the whole phenomenon in terms of light, rather than perception. The eighteenth century, indeed, signals the end of the ancient world of colors, bleaching that world into nothingness with its normalization of perceptual indexes. From now on, there would be a different way of seeing and perceiving colors because there would be an entirely different way of producing them, with the birth of a modern industry of chemical colors on the horizon, looming over the back room of the old dyeshop with its rare, dyed garments and its antiquated trade in privilege.

The particle theory of light, which Newton's conclusive experiments had in certain ways lifted into prominence over the wave theory held quite vigorously by Robert Hooke, placed an emphasis on a certain Cartesian, mechanistic materiality of light. Yet the universe created by Gottfried Wilhelm Leibnitz through differential calculus propounded light as a pure abstraction of frequency, or function, in order to make it the object of calculation, an operation then extended to estimate the speed of light, an estimation made possible only by the speculative mechanics of Jean Foucault and Armand-Hyppolite Fizeau (1849). In a Newtonian way, one began to speak, discreetly, of particles with the largest dimension constituting the red band and those of the smallest dimension the violet band. The mixture of intermediate colors resulted in white (even though the mixture of the entire spectrum actually resulted in gray) and was assumed to be a lack of material qualities so that no "ordering principle" could be discovered, both chromatic and physical, which would render matter as scientifically worthy of study as the phenomenon of light. The additive or subtractive qualities of complementary colors—by definition those that when added to the primary colors result in white—are the "leaps" that color, as a material phenomenon, manages to achieve in its effort to become closer to the ideal phenomenon of light.

6

Action Colors and Passion Colors

GOETHE mounted a campaign of radical opposition to Newton's *Optiks*. Though known most widely as a poet, he was sufficiently skilled at observing the very culture that exalted Newton to be not completely devoted to the idea of the phenomenon, but rather more interested in the subjectivity of the viewer. His *Farbenlehre* and related writings would absorb his attention at least as much as *Faust*, and, curiously, are very much in tune with the drama. Moreover, color theory would prove to have deceived its own author, who held it to be his principal work and, since he had devoted so much time to it, the one most dear to him. He decisively disputed the fundamentality of white light and the serial nature of chromatic sensations, stripping the former of its transparent but durable scientific shell while holding up the latter as the basis for rebuilding a physiognomy/physiology of visual perception by way of the subjectivity/objectivity of the viewer and a comparison between the two parallel functions of physical colors and those created through applied chemistry. Goethe's *Theory of Colors*, downgraded by literary critics to a work of purely specialist interest, became a theoretical workhorse in the new romantic world of ideas and, with relation to the ever-present discussion in his century concerning the "laws of movement and color," represents the first criticism of Enlightenment's positivism from one within the movement who did not wish to build simultaneously a fortress for romantic irrationality. In this way, this authentic encyclopedia on the material nature of colors, like a great continent, spans at the same time the dizzy heights of a love for reason and a fear of its extremes.

Zur Farbenlehre (1808), by which the apodictic and didactic part of the work is generally known and which was most widely circulated and discussed, cannot be separated from the structural part of the work, which has been all but ignored: *Materialien für Geschichte der Farbenlehre* (1810) is important to *Theory of Colors* because of both its luminosity and the shadow it casts on the discussion, which, like light, illuminates colors' "expression and suffering." Perhaps one could see *Farbenlehre* as simply another version of *Faust*, since, indeed, after a rather inconclusive debate on optics (1791) de rigueur for an Enlightenment scholar, a passion for colors seemed to seize Goethe in the course of a unique and extreme existential crisis in 1792, when he was "invited" to follow Charles Augustus, duke of Weimar, and participate in the catastrophic defeat of the highly disciplined Prussian army by the ragtag band led by General Dumouriez, near Valmy. This episode, confronting him with the disastrous results of war and endangering his own life, led Goethe to distract himself philosophically with extemporaneous observations at the edge of a pool of calm water where a ceramic shard lay at the bottom, producing phenomena of light and color.

I cast a glance around me on the field where we were encamped, which was covered with tents up to the hills. On the great, vast green carpet, a strange sight caught my eye: several soldiers sat in a circle and were busy with something in the middle of them. Coming closer to look, I saw that they were squatting around a funnel-shaped hole full of the purest water from a spring whose opening may have been around thirty feet in diameter. Innumerable small fish swam about inside, which the soldiers were fishing after by hook, having brought the necessary tools with them for just such a purpose, along with the rest of their baggage. The water was the clear-est in the world, and the spectacle of this expedition rather amusing. Observing the game, I soon realized that the fish reflected various colors as they moved. At first I thought this phenomenon was due to the chang-ing colors of these little moving bodies, but then I quickly came upon a more satisfactory explanation. In the funnel had fallen a shard of ceramic pottery, which, on the bottom, shone forth with the most beautiful col-ors of the prism. Clear toward the bottom and jutting upward, it presented me, on the opposite edge, with colors of blue and violet, while from the side turned toward me with red and yellow. When, having observed this, I walked around the spring, I saw that the phe-nomenon followed me, and the colors I saw were always the same, as is natural in such subjective experiments.

For me, who had been so taken up with such ques-tions, it was a great pleasure to see here, beneath the sky, in such a clear and natural form, a phenomenon reproduced for which physics professors for over one hundred years had been shutting themselves and their pupils up in darkened rooms. I procured a bit of pottery, which I threw in the well, and could see quite plainly that the phenomenon occurred just as the shard sank below the water's surface, that it became clearer as the shard fell deeper, and that finally, having become but a small white body, shot through with color, it reached the bottom looking for all the world like a tiny flame. Then I remembered that Agricola had already reflected upon this fact and had been induced to classify it as a phenomenon of combustion.[1]

As a throng of thirsty horses broke up the experiment by diving into the small mirror of clear water, Goethe was reminded of the dark outcome of that brutal war, which dirtied both water and life, throwing him out of his dreamworld of colors back into the terror of retreat beneath the volleys of cannons.

The *Theory of Colors* brings together a fragmentary world of colors through a parataxic organization, brief aphorisms strung together like beads of glass both transparent and opaque. This desultory work is thus born, even for its author, out of an experience of insufficiency, and from this compendium of unpredictable proverbs Goethe succeeds in affirming (here the fortunes of nascent idealism are to be found) a dialectical foundation of knowledge open to nature, which moves between opacity and transparency in a synthesis of colors, not in terms of a natural science, but rather as a body of philosophical knowledge that has arisen from the same gray mixture of matter and not from the fictitious unity of Newton's white light: in other words, by way of hidden artistic effort. Color is indistinctly connected to light and to darkness, to black and to white, which when mixed create gray: gray, therefore, and not white, is the color that brings together and forms the basis for all other colors. Light and colors are in a close relationship to each other, but both together are the fruit of a natural completeness that can be seen, not through our sense of sight, but only through experience. Goethe lays out and organizes his work into three parts, the fundamental chapters of his theory: colors manifest themselves *physiologically*, as with subjective colors mediated solely by the perceiving subject; *physically*, as with subjective or objective colors of varying intensity, fleeting or stable, obtainable solely through the imposition of transparent, translucent, or reflective bodies or combinations thereof; and *chemically*, as with more precisely objective colors, fixed on bodies or substances through natural or artificial means.

We can imagine that Goethe's own predilection ran toward physiological colors, in which there is less axiomatic material to be mined, even though these do in fact reveal two fundamental considerations for the future observations on colors: first, that of "consecutive contrast," the chromatic memory that occurs between complementary colors, for example (violet seems to call forth yellow, orange blue, red green, and vice versa), a juxtaposition that gives place to the complete-

ness of chromatic synthesis between the two colors; and, second, that of "simultaneous contrast" when contiguous colors
reveal reciprocal affinity or antipathy, becoming darker or
lighter according to the chromatic strength of one or the other
(as when violet next to blue seems lighter and tends toward
red, while the same shade of violet against an orange background would appear darker, with a tendency toward blue,
just as green on a blue background would appear lighter than
when appearing on an orange background, where it appears
considerably darker and somewhat bluish). Physiological colors, produced in such uncertain ways through the play of light
and shadow, form a subject that excited curious reflections
even in the minds of such pure thinkers as Hegel (*Aphorisms of
Jena*, 1803–6).

> Experiment: The shadow projected by *the light of a can-
> dle* and lit by the *natural light* of morning, becomes blue;
> the shadow thrown by the light of day (the shadow
> which is the weakest, created by distancing oneself from
> the light) and illuminated by the light of a candle, be-
> comes red. The shadow thrown by the light of a candle,
> when the object is held close to the candle, flickers
> greenish.[2]

Physiological colors force upon the fundamental designations
of colors a principle of perceptual deformation or pathology—
for example, the lack of blue perception for acyanobleptics, in
place of which these individuals see a very faded purple, or the
visual defect that causes a perception of images smeared with

yellow (cropsy), or those blinding, intolerable spots of light that warn of brain damage.

In Goethe's physical colors we find the clearest response to Newton, for in these reside the reductive psychological influences on values of tints in their passage and transference through the means of optical phenomena. Dioptric colors, those seen with the aid of a simple glass prism and accorded the privilege of scientific observations, are listed by Goethe alongside other chromatic phenomena: catoptric (reflected) colors, paroptic (perioptic) colors, epoptic colors, and finally, entoptic colors. All these are the conditions experienced by Goethe in classifying colors relative to the appearance of the phenomenon of physical colors. Finally, chemical colors close his discussion and are presented as chromatic phenomena that cannot be seen apart from their own history or the form in which they were produced by unstable methods: through generation, intensification, inversion, fixation, and mixture, alongside the various powers colors have possessed through time, cultural history, science, and philosophy.

The didactic part of *Theory of Colors* concludes with the chapter that, somewhat irrationally, brings together opinions and interpretations from the "theory of form" and the "psychology of perception." Here it is a question of the "symbolic and moral action of color," which enlarges the didactic aspect of his work into the prophetic and therapeutic mode of Ruldolph Steiner, using a body of knowledge, at once erudite and commonplace, on the original sensations that colors and their forms have always evoked. Goethe writes:

Since colour occupies so important a place in the series
of elementary phenomena, filling as it does the limited
circle assigned to it with fullest variety, we shall not be
surprised to find that its effects are at all times decided
and significant, and that they are immediately associated
with the emotions of the mind. We shall not be surprised to find that these appearances present singly, are
specific, that in combination they may produce an harmonious, characteristic, often even an inharmonious effect on the eyes, by means of which they act on the
mind; producing this impression in their most general
elementary character, without relation to the nature or
form of the object on whose surface they are apparent.
Hence, colour considered as an element of art, may be
made subservient to the highest aesthetical ends.

759: People experience a great delight in colour, generally. The eye requires it as much as it requires light.
We have only to remember the refreshing sensation we
experience, if on a cloudy day the sun illumines a single
portion of the scene before us and displays its colours.
That healing powers were ascribed to coloured gems,
may have arisen from the experience of this indefinable
pleasure.

760: The colours which we see on objects are not
qualities entirely strange to the eye; the organ is not thus
merely habituated to the impression; no, it is always
predisposed to produce colour of itself, and experiences
a sensation of delight if something analogous to its own
nature is offered to it from without; if its susceptibility
is distinctly determined towards a given state.

761: From some of our earlier observations we can
conclude, that general impressions produced by single

colours cannot be changed, that they act specifically, and must produce definite, specific states in the living organ.

762: They likewise produce a corresponding influence on the mind. Experience teaches us that particular colours excite particular states of feeling. It is related of a witty Frenchman, "Il prétendoit que son ton de conversation avec Madame étoit changé depuis qu'elle avoit changé en cramoisi le meuble de son cabinet, qui étoit bleu."

763: In order to experience these influences complete, the eye should be entirely surrounded with one colour; we should be in a room of one colour, or look through a coloured glass. We are then identified with the hue, it attunes the eye and mind in mere unison with itself. The colours on the *plus* side are yellow, red-yellow (orange), yellow-red (minium, cinnabar). The feelings they excite are quick, lively, aspiring. . . .

765: *Yellow.* This is the colour nearest the light. It appears on the slightest migration of light, whether by semi-transparent mediums or faint reflection from white surfaces. In prismatic experiments, it extends itself alone and widely in the light space, and while the two poles remain separated from each other, before it mixes with blue to produce green it is to be seen in its utmost purity and beauty. How the chemical yellow develops itself in and upon the white, has been circumstantially described in its proper place.

766: In its highest purity it always carries with it the nature of brightness, and has a serene, gay, softly exciting character. . . .

778: *Blue.* As yellow is always accompanied with

light, so it may be said that blue still brings a principle of darkness with it.

779: This colour has a peculiar and almost indescribable effect on the eye. As a hue it is powerful, but it is on the negative side, and in its highest purity is, as it were, a stimulating negation. Its appearance, then, is a kind of contradiction between excitement and repose. . . .

792: *Red.* We are here to forget everything that borders on yellow or blue. We are to imagine an absolutely pure red, like fine carmine suffered to dry on white porcelain.

793. Whoever is acquainted with the prismatic origin of red, will not think it paradoxical if we assert that this colour partly *actu*, partly *potentia*, includes all the other colours. . . .

801: *Green.* If yellow and blue, which we consider as the most fundamental and simple colours, are united as they first appear, in the first state of their action, the colour which we call green is the result.

802: The eye experiences a distinctly grateful impression from this colour. If the two elementary colours are mixed in perfect equality so that neither predominates, the eye and the mind repose on the result of this junction as upon a simple colour. The beholder has neither the wish nor the power to imagine a state beyond it. Hence for rooms to live in constantly, the green colour is most generally selected."[3]

As we have indicated, the most important suggestion contained in this didactic section became the keystone for the theory of visual perception up until recent years and was the classic text of the practical experimentation carried out by the Bauhaus school of Walter Gropius; those artists most concerned with colored materials, including Johannes Itten, Josef Albers, Wassily Kandinsky, and Paul Klee; and Vchutemas and Vhcutein, the technical-artistic state studios of Rodchenko and N. T. Federov in Moscow. Indeed, the psychological interpretation of color seemed to prevail over others such as the physiological, which in reality was closer to Goethe's thinking and was represented by the historical side of the discussion, which constitutes a brilliant and comprehensive encyclopedia of discourses and forms of colors. In this part of his work are listed the relevant writings according to author, along with all the hard, bitter insights of analytical and philosophical knowledge concerning a subject so near to experience and so far from theory. The result is an analysis and archeology of chromatic knowledge and of the disciplinary "directorial" techniques of these very sciences in grappling with a subject whose contours are revelatory and difficult to define. If the didactic section of *Farbenlehre* was perhaps exploited in the quest for a psychology of vision, a reevaluation of the historical part ought to acknowledge it, not precisely as epistemology and thus neither as an aesthetic theory on the appearance of forms, but as the first book on the history of the techniques and uses of colors, an object of study as difficult to legitimize and contain between two cultures as the vast, well-disciplined, and relative field of colors.

Goethe's theory of colors excited the enthusiasm of Schopenhauer and the admiration of Beethoven. His scheme

of primary colors (blue, yellow, and purple) proposed intermediate mixtures of red-yellow and red-blue tending in ascent
(figure 2) toward purple (a color both ancient and mythic)
and thus giving rise to green as an inferior result and a natural
combination.

Hegel was as fiercely interested in this schema as were Otto
Runge and the Nazarene painters, who interpreted, with
Goethe, the mission of traveling to Italy as one of fervid contemplation of one state of colors: the tension of Italic red
corrected by Germanic colors—yellow, blue and therefore
green (as in the painting *Italie und Deutschland* by Friedrich
Overbeck).

Goethe's commentary on physiological colors announced
his objective, however inchoate, to create an a priori synthesis of physical
and chemical colors.
Though Goethe's
organic perspective
was simply a deriv-
ative of Enlight-
enment naturalism,
one can spot in his
thinking the distinc-
tions concerning the
thoroughly debated
question of the ob-
jectivity or subjec-
tivity of knowledge,

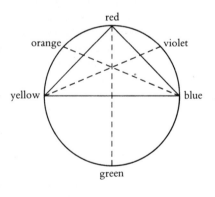

FIGURE 2

just as elsewhere the brilliant Newtonian Francesco Algarotti had already outlined for artists the difficulties of the very theories which he propounded (1762): "Colors are not otherwise innate to light; on the contrary, they are but modifications that light undergoes in the act of its reflection or transmission through bodies, being subjected to endless changes and lost in infinity."[4]

In Goethe, however, one can still find ingenious observations and considerations on the preservation of colors on the retina, a phenomenon that to him seemed to threaten the spontaneity and independence of the visual faculty. This, according to his way of thinking, should have served to prove the existence of perception rather than deny it, since here was the apparatus that enables the perception of movement but does so through the objects that surround us like fleeting, fleeing colors.

The aspect of Goethe's theory of greatest interest, though, is not his intended defeat of the science of physics, which had reached a point of theorizing in an absolute way using partial and uncertain observations. Rather, it lies in his opening the way, quite unexpectedly, toward the applied science of chemistry, a science wholly lacking in any historical interest in scientific operations beyond the means used to support its own theoretical propositions. Indeed, the historical perspective on a theory of colors would come to fall within the outlines of a critical elaboration of the system of perception, which, I believe, constitutes a turning away from the absolutistic color-blind faith in scientific "powers of observation."

Scientific method in this sense manufactures historical necessity to create a presumption of absolute truth concerning the social order to which it belongs and to which it is connected in every way, however small: such is the case of chemical production in the industrial age.

Only through Goethe can one discern, among artistic techniques, the relationships between the various sensibilities in the visual arts and a reemergence of attention to the system of production and their own internal conceptual functioning. Gottfried Semper, for example, found the research material for his "Origin of Polychromy" (1854)[5] among the populations of the world, proposing the simple weaving of baskets and mats as the beginning of all production techniques. His position is certainly grafted upon Goethe's cultural organicism more solidly than Conrad Fiedler's "pure visibility" as the perceptual abstraction of forms inherent in matter. In any case, these two principal derivations that sprang up alongside Goethe's theories on colors enjoyed success, along with Gestalt psychology and the classificatory disciplines of visual perception, which, as material and cultural history and within its own invented tradition, tied together families of objects, like thoughts, in the design and the forms of expressive architecture.

7

The Color of Color

IN eighteenth- and nineteenth-century France, ongoing experimentation in dyeing and weaving was the legacy of the government's sponsorship of the decorative arts, as at the Gobelins, a Parisian dye and tapistry works in existence from the fifteenth century to the present. Among that legacy was the politician Jean-Baptiste Colbert's establishment in 1671 of a code of quality standards: "All visible things are distinguished and made desirable through color. It is not enough that the colors be beautiful for trade in cloth to thrive; the dyestuff must also be of high quality, so that it lasts as long as the goods in which it is used. Nature shows us the difference and should be our example: she uses a weak color for flowers, which soon fade, but uses a different color for grass, metals, and precious gems, where she uses a stronger shade and colors them according to the length of their lifetime."[1] This code was intended to organize the dye trade and to strengthen its most desirable branches through the regulation and inspection of dye production and distribution of goods. Manuals like the *Instructions* of Charles-François Du Fay and others on the dyemaker's art should thus be seen in this light, as should the guidance on boiling techniques and wool and cloth work provided by J. Hellot (1750). Such treatises, typical of the Enlightenment, collected beneath their rigorous economic nomenclature a mass of practical recipes and formulas no longer useful to the "Pays de Cocagne" (the land of plenty), the term used to describe countries with huge stockpiles of seasoned dyestuff in reserve, sold on the black market as a nontaxable asset.

Alongside regulatory interventions concerning the territorial production of the dye trade was the gradual discovery and substitution of aniline dyes. The production of these dyes grew enormously during the nineteenth century, and aniline dyes remain a standard representing the highest color value imparted to raw thread. If women—so said the traders—had preferred from the beginning white cotton over red, the textile industry would have grown steadily and overcome one of the primary obstacles to its growth. To have had a single regulation that would have guaranteed the uniform production of dyes next door to the place where the cloth was woven would have resolved many problems without having to rely upon the uncertain substitution of natural dyes produced through cultivation. The chemical industry's major effort was not only to produce dyes to match the various scales of natural colors already in use according to popular taste and appearance but to promote these products as more convenient and thereby eliminate de facto that which was rare, dear, or unique. When people began to see and dress in different colors, they began to think differently as well.

Along with the regulation of dyestuffs, Enlightenment scientists made continuing efforts to determine what chromatic perceptions were abnormal or defective. John Dalton, by analyzing his own color blindness, proposed that anomalies of chromatic perception usually fell within the red range, a phenomenon afterward acknowledged to include blue and violet as well, though these are physiologically less common. An important discussion of this topic in relation to physiological colors was offered again by Goethe, who, in the face of Dalton's *Extraordinary Facts Relating to the Vision of Colours* (1794), proposed a program of post-Newtonian research on "achromatopsia," complete color blindness. This phenomenon had been analyzed by Dollond and Westfeld in terms of retinal images and by Robert Waring Darwin in terms of the perseveration of images and colors perceived by subjects.

The various efforts of science and chemistry to create profitable applications of Newton's mostly theoretical work on colors led to a reexamination of the production of classic dyes in the ancient world. Those practices, by now entirely extinct, in fact gave rise to industrial techniques of immediate practical application, for example, in the process of fixation—that is, preparing the cloth to receive the dye—and in whitewashing the bleaching or lixiviation of thread or cloth. Thus developed a vast purgative process that aimed to eliminate all dirt and any traces of the weaving process along with the natural colors of the cloth so as to ready the material for administration of the coloring agent. The moral tone of hygiene and cleanliness would be imposed socially in the civilizing influence of the "white" man, as can be discerned by a group of manuals on such specific topics as *Experiments on Bleaching* (1756), *Experiments upon Magnesia Alba* (1756), and *Description du blanchiment des toiles* (1785). Submersion into baths and washing with ashes, old whitening techniques using sulfur and niter known since classical times and handed down in domestic lore, now needed vast space on high hills to lay out the cloth to whiten, a practice that surprised the Continental traveler who came across the extraordinarily white fields of Manchester. This, however, was still a bleaching industry taking place outside the factory, using agricultural lands, and was soon to be replaced in industrial development first by dyeing and then by bleaching powder (1798), hailed as a victory for the middle class, who both wore and sold household linens and who thereby overcame any Jacobin "sansculotte" and civilized the shirtless "savage."

The unceasing efforts of industry and chemical invention slowly laid the groundwork for the synthetic production of color, which began to obtain high-quality results of maximum durability, resistant to wear and to nearly any kind of destructive agent over time. Then in the beginning of the twentieth century, "indantrene" dyes were developed, creating a river of artificial color before which all delicate, ancient colors paled.

Centers of industrial production were located primarily in continental Europe, Germany in particular, while in England the textile industry had long preferred to import dyestuffs from the colonies (indigo from Antilles) and so was limited in its development of a chemical dye industry. In 1839 Friedrich

Engels in *Letters from Wuppertal* depicted the profound transformation of his birthplace, comparing the ancient labor of
bleaching on fields of grass to the new modern industry of
dyes that colored and polluted rivers and countryside: "The
narrow stream sometimes flows quickly, sometime slug-
gishly, its purple ripples in the midst of smoky factories and
bleachworks covered with cloth. Its reddish color comes not
from some bloody battle . . . nor even from shame at the
actions of men, though such a motive could certainly be understood, but rather solely and exclusively from the many
dyeworks producing Turkey red."[2] Turkey red at the beginning of the nineteenth century still required a complicated
process of manufacture that used a base of madder and en-
tailed numerous separate operations: the removal of any
woody debris from the cotton, submersion into manure to
"roughen" the fiber and make it more amenable to coloring
agents, oiling and bleaching, removal of oily substances
through warm soda baths, tanning with gall from oak and
sumac, treatment with alum, application of a fixative, a bath
to remove the alum and the fixative, and then a repetition of
the final steps from bleaching to the treatment with alum.
Then the actual process of dyeing began: as the material was
boiled in the essence of madder, ox or ram's blood was added
and the skein was wrung out and then washed. The bright-
ening operation followed this, using oil or soap, and then the
perfecting of the tint was carried out using tin salts or nitric
acid, with successive rinsing in boiling soapy water.

This process survived in the traditional manufacturing regions that were rich in water. By the second half of the nine-teenth century, however, artificial alizarine, first synthesized in 1868 to replace madder tincture, facilitated a greatly sim-plified process for obtaining Turkey red, which had retained its place as the longest-lasting but also the most difficult and costly color to produce. Consequently, there began a decline in the cultivation of madder, the oldest and best-known dye-producing plant, whose topographical designations (*robbia, rubia,* or *rosées,* in Italian, Spanish, and French, respectively) still were used to denote several regions in Tuscany and Sicily, Alsace and southern France, Thuringia and Saxony. These names still connoted a high quality of merchandise or garment (*roba-e,* signifying "stuff" in Romance languages).

Thus, one can understand how the numerous public com-petitions and national prizes offered for the discovery of the simplest and most durable red dye became almost literally a civil campaign in favor of artificial dyes and succeeded in drawing forth local secrets into a centralized system of pro-duction, a deal concluded under the Second Empire in its monopoly on red dye, used for army-regulation trousers. Among these flasks of colors, therefore, began a new chapter in organic chemistry when the claim was made that only or-ganic life could produce organic substances in the face of the distillation and synthesis of vegetable and animal extracts used in dye making, such as artificial urine.

Following the appearance of malveine, aniline, and fucsin, all red dyes, the creation of artificial indigo in 1880 could be seen as the endpoint of the nineteenth century's experimental crusade in color production, begun with the Enlightenment adventurism of Napoleon's minister Jean-Antoine Chaptal. And yet France, which held the record for discoveries of single coloring agents, soon found itself surpassed by the German chemical industry, which by the end of the century produced nearly all synthetic coloring agents and dyes. This situation arose out of the development of such companies as Bayer, Hoechst, and Ciba (known at that time as Friedrich Bayer & Co., Farbwerke Meister Lucius und Bruning at Hoechst, and la Société pour l'industrie chimique à Bâle, respectively), whose success rested solely on the production of dyes and distribution of synthetically produced colors. The industry then began to grow to gigantic proportions thanks to a significant development: the enormous production of coloring agents was transformed into the production of explosives (such as orange-yellow coloring agents using niter), which in turn resulted in today's pharmaceutical industry. Was it not Aristotle, Theophrastus, and Dioscurides who considered color (*chroma*) a drug (*pharmakon*)?

In the course of a century and a half, the chemical industry's products soon were completely interrelated: dyes and colors, explosives, drugs, and foods. Such a development had been anticipated in Edward Bancroft's design for textile production, which had touted throughout eighteenth-century Europe and America the virtues of dyeing agents based on *khaki* (derived from quercitron, the bark of the American black oak), which had been the object of scientific research (1794) carried out with a single thought inspired by color: "the philosophy of permanent color."

The use of hygienic white, which became current in the eighteenth century, presupposed a more or less Newtonian pragmatism in which all other colors were considered in the light of a clear, civilizing mind-set, extending into shadowy areas an overpowering effort toward cleanliness. Still, such a white certainty could not escape the profound ambiguity Melville found in the pursuit of his white monster, Moby Dick (1850):

> Or is it, that as in essence whiteness is not so much a color as the visible absence of color; and at the same time the concrete of all colors; is it for these reasons that there is such a dumb blankness, full of meaning, in a wide landscape of snows—a colorless, all-color of athe-ism from which we shrink? And when we consider that other theory of the natural philosophers, that all other earthly hues . . . are but subtle deceits, not actually in-herent in substances, but only laid on from without; so that all deified Nature absolutely paints like the harlot, whose allurement covers nothing but the charnel-house within; when we proceed further, and consider that the mystical cosmetic which produces every one of her hues, the great principle of light, for ever remains white or colorless in itself . . . pondering all this, the palsied universe lies before us like a leper."[3]

In this manner, even Rabelais in *Gargantua*, with his white clothes in the midst of "pious black," sounded an unexpected call among natural colors for the hypnotic qualities of white:

the lion, whose roar frightens all animals on earth, itself fears and shows respect for only the white chicken.

In this period of uncertainty and debate, white as a phenomenon becomes absolutized not solely with respect to light but with respect to darkness as well, which, in the opinion of Goethe and the romantic writers, can exist only in poetry and painting: thus was born a new topic of artistic production, the chiaroscuro, a drawing permeated by dimming light and by a color that becomes fixed in the form of the objects depicted (monochrome and grisaille). More generally, from the "air color" that had dominated the facades of eighteenth-century cities, white began to reign, a throwback to neoclassical fantasies embodied in the cemeteries of the bourgeoisie, who marked with white its separation from the black and smoky reality of the working classes. The white of classicist marbles is adopted by the nineteenth-century city as an archeological, historical, and social principle designed to ennoble buildings and public and private furnishings, whereas for the classical Greeks the inexpressive quality of white would have robbed everything of value. This is evidenced by the polychrome decorations of the Parthenon, the sparkling, colored limbs of Olympian statuary, the rainbow eyes of classical statues, which were never white until neoclassicism saw them that way. The classical-white recitations preferred by bourgeois society, with its taste for melodrama, adopted a historic convention based not on the actual archeological truth but rather on a fantasied appearance that could promulgate the new ethos of liberty, equality, and property rights consecrated by the

French Revolution. This somewhat dubious way of thinking, applied to the decoration of buildings according to a new national destiny, grew even more prominent in the general whitening of interiors, meant to clean the slate of all visible traces of the past so as to make way for a new inhabitability, erasing all signs of previous human occupation in the hope of being able to create a new and different way of life. In white and in limestone were interred all mourning and memory of tragedy, creating within these very walls the possibility for the new energy and new hopes of the bourgeoisie: health, work, family.

Alongside this effort to whiten both public and private spaces to make place for the new ambience of the egalitarian, bourgeois city, an individual, personal black came into wide use in furnishings and clothing like a spiky exoskeleton, as this charming letter from eighteenth-century Venice demonstrates:

> Say what you will, but silkworms and the color black are the two most praiseworthy things in the world. Let the sheep and all other living creatures who give their coat and skin to man so that he may clothe himself go and hide. You will think me mad to say such things to you so readily, but I am in rapturous love with a black cloak that I used for masquerade. The first day I had disembarked, I posed with a mask in a woolen coat of a certain color tending toward brown, because there was a strong west wind that hurt my innards, and I went out of the house that way so that no one would stop me and chat. I become aware that, in walking the streets, there

was neither gentleman nor workman who did not wish to pass in front of me and who, in passing, did not elbow me in the chest. I could not repeat to you the shouts that an accountant hurled at me, the curses that were thrown at me, such that I returned home quite dismayed and more than a little livid and bruised. Quite aware of the great stream of people who come and go, up and down, here and there, I went out the next morning in another coat of scarlet hue. Nearly the same occurred to me as had the previous day, and I returned to the inn where I was lodging, bruised and pushed about like a grape in the vat. The innkeeper, who had heard me sighing and groaning in the vestibule in great affliction, asked me what was wrong. "Dear fellow," said I, "I have paid my way to enjoy the remainder of carnival in a good bed and a well-padded mattress in your inn. I find in every street a crowd of people coming and going with such fury that I am at a loss to protect myself from blows in every direction, such that I return to the inn with marks about my ribs and arms. If everyone returns to their houses in similar state, you all must use an ocean of ointment in this town."

The innkeeper laughed and answered me, saying, "My dear sir, this is all your own fault, if you'll pardon my saying so, for going about with two coats that attract and invite ill manners on the part of all whom you pass in town."

"My coats?" said I. "But they have only yesterday left the hands of the tailor who made them."

"Do as you wish," he replied, "but if you do not own a black silken coat, you run the risk of coming home with a broken back or legs."

Accepting the advice of my good innkeeper, I quickly had myself made a neat black cloak that shone like a looking glass, and I went out wearing it. Wonder of wonders, if I was not quickly in the midst of the crowd of people, and whomever was in back of me stayed in back, while those beside me merely brushed gingerly past such that I felt all but alone in the crowd. From that point on, I sought revenge for all the proddings I had received by doing the same to all who did not wear a cloak such as mine. It is true that I am not as comfortable as I was in my other two coats and feel the cold, but one cannot have everything in life. I warn you of what happened to me, knowing that you are to come to Venice soon, so that you will dress accordingly. I am wholly yours in friendship in respect.[4]

In the same way red, the color of the army and of battle, slowly began to acquire certain ideological connotations from popular revolutions, retained even today. On the other hand, the intellectual aestheticism of the English pre-Raphaelite movements would dress itself in "green and yellow melancholy," wishing to avoid the choice between the black path of the cleric or the red path of the warrior, a choice indicated by the title of Stendhal's novel *The Red and the Black*. Nevertheless, an intimate connection between the colors of red and black would persist when the modern world began to develop new variants and attributions, seeing in these colors feelings of aggression or signs of mourning.

In nineteenth-century society, as in the symbolism of heraldry from an earlier time, color seemed to acquire a certain powerful influence, though it was not as precisely regulated by codes as it was in manuals of chivalry and guild records. Tricolor flags were raised as demonstrations of unity and national ideals achieved, consecrated once again to a resurgence of popular patriotism. In the same manner, the colored uniforms of the armed forces were able to dress entire populations who now, as individuals and citizens, could possess, along with colored clothing, a homeland and a destiny—though the fact was not mentioned that in the art of war, the multicolor chessboard of troops in a battlefield served the purpose of distinguishing formations and thus anticipating incursions and assaults. The distinction of military colors, in the midst of the green of the countryside, was above all an offensive maneuver, seeming to amplify the number of troops: it was a preferred tactic to reveal openly the numerical force of one's troops, and, reciprocally, the ratio of attack and the direction of the encounter as an exchange of colored targets. One should thus remember, in this regard, that Napoleon's great battles were a betrayal of classical "chromatic" tactics until the tragic epilogue of the battle of Sebastopol. The military use of color would move on from this point, gradually, along the opposite front: the obvious individuation of colored formations of an army or its aggressive components would, instead, become a tool for invisibility and would serve to mask any movement or appearance that might be too revealing: simulation and surprise would become more and more decisive as the wartime display, meant to signal and extend the army and the infantry, became even more aggressive when adorned with their own colors.

The use of military camouflage during World War I came from colonial usage, since that was the way colonial armies of the late nineteenth century were dressed, in colors ranging from dark green to khaki, colors of lower military ranks. The typical colors of World War I uniforms, spotted with a mixture of earthy greens, browns, and grays, enabled soldiers to crawl along the ground and be lost in the underbrush. Meanwhile, more distinctive colors began to appear on the helmets and insignias of companies and platoons with history and tradition. Vestigial decorations, such as tassels, piping, and stripes, were sewn onto a uniform background of gray-green (in place of the blue, white, and red uniforms of a previous era) and introduced into the lining of helmets and the finish of weapons, carrying with them all the risks and consequences that come from indistinguishability, especially when unexpected mass movements of people on land and at night create possible targets for the enemy. The mimetic needs of war, more or less comparable to the chameleonism of plants or animals, would end up spotting every motorized vehicle, once the obligatory black, with a military coloration. Similarly, ships were given a mottled appearance to reduce their visibility (dazzle painting). An uncertainty still hung in the air between distinctive or mimetic coloration for the new aircraft, due to the basic problem of visibility against a background of varying colors: land, water, sky. As military objects colored in camouflage had to carry distinguishing wartime insignias or a circle with the national flag—that is, declarative, unequivocal colors—even the vaulting wooden airplane would soon become a colored warhorse in the fray. Such camouflage was not used for peacetime signs or vehicles or for those designated to give aid, which instead were marked with the sign of untouchability—white—and with the European-Christian red cross of peacemaking taken from the ancient flag of surrender, calling to mind the yellow flag raised during epidemics and times of quarantine, which by their very nature repelled any possible offensive action.

White, as the union of all colors—even with its ambiguities—and black, with its negative connotations, became widely used in industrial cities precisely because of their absence of color. With their popularity there came about a re-installation of individuation between each color, dark and light, light and dark. The selection of colors tended to become uniform in the medium range of inoffensive, neutral colors and grays. This uniformity did not have a direct effect on the use of colors or on the manufacture of objects, but rather was a process of ever-changing, eloquent identification of each color with an object: colors of the homeland, in the flag, for instance; or colors of fashion or representation in clothes; or colors of art in paintings; colors of the field in the garden. In this way, the range of colors used by society, provoking thoughts and behaviors within a unified web of precise rules of conformity, became in fact a predetermined "object" of sorts. Variation becomes swallowed by uniqueness when white and black come to depict joy or grief, the troubles of life, or objectives successfully reached, or when black, used in the eighteenth century in masquerades and costuming, comes to be defined as the color of respect, widow's weeds in the wardrobe of the bourgeoisie. A certain individuality is expressed in the use of pink or blue for babies as distinctive signals of sex during infancy, the instructive color of that "little homeland" which is the family. Infancy is thus a continent of colors, in its play of "instinctive rhythms" which Rimbaud speaks of in his poem *Vowels*: *A* black, *E* white, *I* red, *O* blue, *U* green.[5]

8

Colors and Color Theory

OUR ABILITY to see in color (as opposed to seeing the individual colors themselves) comes about through processes of addition and subtraction (researched by Maxwell), an understanding of which facilitates the reproduction and transmission of colors. Both processes begin with the premise that there are three primary colors, which can be combined to form all others. These colors are arranged in groups and by type—red, blue, green, cyan, magenta, yellow—and as such are subject to two types of operations: the first corresponds to colors transmitted via light (additive phenomena), the second is based on mixture or superimposition (subtractive phenomena). In brief, the first is produced through projecting the three primary colors on a white screen (figure 3) in the form of a circle, obtaining in this way through simple superimposition the three colors (cyan, magenta, yellow), which, when translucent circles of colored paper are laid over them in the manner shown in figure 4, yield the three original colors used (red, blue, green), with black appearing in the middle in place of white.

One might expect painters, because they use pigments, to have been most interested in Maxwell's experiments in subtractive synthesis. However, pointillist painters like Georges

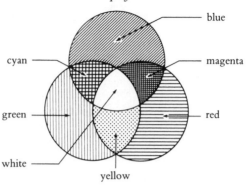

FIGURE 3

Seurat, who rejected traditional combinations, used Max-well's discovery with the intention of creating an effect of *additive* synthesis by allowing the viewer's eye to combine small dots of pure color to form larger areas of complex colors. The pointillists also made use of Goethe's discovery, seconded by the chemist Michel-Eugène Chevreul, concerning the effects of adjacent colors on color perception.

In addition to the effects obtained by mixing lights and pigments, considerations concerning chromatic recall and contrasts (red/green, yellow/blue) are both the least and the most that can be proven in a theory of colors. This remains so even after establishing the principles that govern retinal reception and the transmission of chromatic stimuli to the brain, not to mention subsequent discoveries concerning chromatic perception, such as automatic coloration (when, for example,

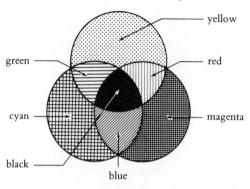

yellow

green

red

cyan

magenta

black

blue

FIGURE 4

a black-and-white image is perceived when a red filter is used, proven by Edwin Land's experiment) or phosphenes (the ir-idescent disks or checkerboard patterns, in color of yellow and violet, green and red, perceived when the eyes are pressed against a pillow).

On the one hand, techniques for reproducing images in the press, by photography, in movies, or on television are evi-dence that technical procedures begin essentially with black and white, a fact that coincides more or less with the color-bind theory behind the applied sciences which makes color a somewhat secondary phenomenon. However, the verisimili-tude of things reproduced in black and white is supported only by an *intellectual* resistance to seeing things in color, since with the same optical equipment—from the simple spyglass telescope to the cathode-ray tube—all-encompassing explosions of color leap at the eye, suggesting another more experiential way of thinking about the world entirely.

Strictly speaking, not even monochromatic photography was originally black and white, though we have gotten used to thinking of it as a shadow on a plate that has been drained white through exposure to light. Actually it was originally gray-white and silver, or sepia and yellow, or snow white and blue, or clear and reddish, depending upon the chemical reactions first used in calotype negatives, or the diffuse, ghostly silver of daguerreotypes. White and black are the colors given to the blank page of xylography, to etching, and to ink printing, colors mediated by the effect of the longer-lasting negative on the photographic plate and thus transferred onto the transparent silhouettes that are given life as the "chères ombres" of the movie theater. In early photography, the artist's brushstrokes made color the finishing, "artistic" touch to a profile or subject already outlined by the camera. One should not think, by these observations, that photographic portraiture enjoyed easy success and immediate acceptance: even if the picture appeared to be a mirror image, the subject often did not recognize his own face in the photograph and indeed did not *want* to recognize himself in black and white, until color, applied to the image like makeup, softened the contours and imitated his natural complexion, thus ironically bringing it into line with the artificial similitude of the painted portrait, which, despite everything, seemed more true to life than the perplexing, "ugly" image in black and white, a mournful simulacrum of an early death.

Louis Ducos du Hauron reintroduced one aspect of painting into the techniques of photographic development and thus "definitively" resolved the problem that color posed for photography: "To make color depict what is seen, with colors prepared exactly as they appear—this is the problem that I have articulated and solved. My procedure, which is an *indirect* procedure, will probably be judged as the only practical system, or at least the most practical among those the future holds."[1]

Impressionist and pointillist painting, up through fauvism and futurism, were no strangers to the chromatic experimentalism of figures like Chevreul or to the development or simple theoretical conceptions concerning perceptions, such as that of "simultaneous contrast," found, for example, in the preabstract madness of Van Gogh, who painted a white wall using white. Abstract painting and cubism, through neoplasticism,[2] in attempting a mystical identification and reunion of the various arts—music, poetry, sculpture, and painting—rediscovered in color a principle of perceptual certainty just as drawing had at one time defined the form and models of art. Kazimir Malevich's painting *Black on White* (1913) and Achille Ricciardi's *Theater of Color* (dated 1920, but actually 1913) lay the basis for the importance attributed to color by an avant-garde seeking a middle road between the twin dangers of suprematism and futurism. The ineffable fate of the "three actions" in Michel Seuphor's theater piece *The Ephemeral Is Eternal*, with three identical and different trichromatic sets by Piet Mondrian, describes both the dullness and chromatic inebriation of these avant-garde dreams.

Wassily Kandisky's *Über Geistige in der Kunst* (On the spiritual in art, 1912) reflects a less axiomatic view of the consonance between the form of colors and musical sounds (azure flute, blue cello); instead, he summarizes with great clarity Goethe's theme of physiological colors, imbuing them with a sensibility that moves toward musical harmony. This parallel with music was already mentioned in 1786 by Johann Leonhard Hoffman in his comparison of visual and aural phenomena,[3] which was intended to correct, through colors, Goethe's deafness to musical effects. That defect was shared by Immanuel Kant, who had relegated arts created by temporal succession or scansion (music, dance, and poetry) to a position inferior to those forms of art in which revelation was instantaneous (painting, architecture, sculpture). Within the sensibility of the Enlightenment (as opposed to that of romanticism) the latter were preferred for the instantaneous enlightenment imparted by the rational effect of artifice over the progressive transport of emotions and passions such as are obtained in the musical theater or the symphony. Yet the attempt to draw parallels between the spatial and temporal arts placed looking and listening within a larger system of perceptual psychology, apparent in Goethe's conception of physiological colors.

In an effort to give form to the mechanism of creation, Scriabin's tone poem *Prometheus* (1908) from the start used a controversial machine as a musical instrument: the *clavier à lumière* or keyboard of light, which produced colors to match sounds according to a prefixed set of correspondences—red for C, violet for C sharp, yellow for D, and so on. Schoenberg's theories in *Farbklangbildt* at the end of *Harmonielehre* (1911) had already been explored by Webern in "Klangfarbenmelodie," one of his *Six Pieces for Orchestra*, op. 6, of 1909. The latter in my opinion resembles Luigi Nono's *Io, a Fragment of Prometheus* (1981), a work cruelly deprived of color (*logos* drives out *chroma*) like a body without insides, beauty without a face. And yet problems remained. Though a correspondence was perceived between sound and color, between the spectrum of sounds and the harmony of colors, in which tint is timbre, brilliance is pitch, and saturation is dynamics, a black hole remained concerning that color without correspondence to sound, namely, shadow, which, to use the parallel, could be nothing but a long, silent pause. Likewise, since among sounds, successive distinctions in colors melt in the blending of tones, the supposedly distinct instantaneous and successive characters of these two fields clash. This brings a discord between two different material worlds of aesthetics, which when taken together are like unpleasant music played backward.

Kandinsky's orchestration of colors is, nevertheless, unique in its didactic authenticity: thus, at the beginning of a chromatic discussion framed in terms of hot and cold, Kandinsky stresses the fundamental aspects of yellow and blue, along with their centrifugal and centripetal force, respectively, in order to evoke archetypal feelings such as corporeity (yellow) and spirituality (blue). Another hot and cold pair, black and white, evoke respectively rebellion against the world, life, and birth, versus passivity, suffering, passage, and death. "White acts upon our psyche like a great silence that for us is absolute" but, like a musical silence, is surrounded by sound and filled with resonance. Black, on the other hand, is a sound which is present as a continuous echo, like a basso ostinato. A third pair, red and green, suggests the juxtaposition of powerful immobility and powerless mobility. A fourth comprises orange, which in its derivation from yellow moves in a centrifugal direction, and violet, which, from blue, moves centripetally. A concentric circle, with blue and yellow at the poles, alternating red and green, violet and orange, rotates in a fixed way, separating at its extremes the opposites of black and white, as in the schema (figure 5) that summarizes *Über Geistige in der Kunst*. In Kandinsky's theater piece *The Sound Yellow* (1912), from a dark background positive lights are unleashed, leading to the birth of the world out of chaos, while in *Violet* (1911–14) reddish lights overlaid with a triangle cause a catastrophe, which in turn causes a renewed principle of generativity to emerge. Following the heat of *Blaue Reiter* (1912), Franz Marc, one of Kandisky's friends, still heard the colored whistling of an aphorism given shape at Verdun: "The ancient faith in colors, through a transcendence of the senses and of matter, will win out in ecstatic fervor and interiority just as, at one time, faith in God won out over the emptiness of the graven image. Color, freed from that which is material, will lead to immanence, through our will."[4]

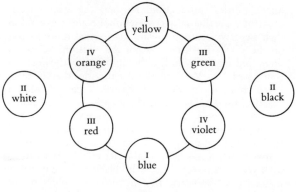

FIGURE 5

While the central ideas of the avant-garde had both the linearity and compelling form of a manifesto, Paul Klee developed his ideas on color circa 1920 through engaging in the particularities of a practice distantly related to sound effects (he, like Kandinsky, considered himself a musician manqué) and modifying the mystical effects of Runge's *Farbenkugel* and Rudolf Steiner's *Essence of Colors*. For conventional color theory he had little use:

> That which most artists have in common, an aversion to color as a science, became understandable to me when, a short time ago, I read Ostwald's theory of colors. I gave myself a little time to see if I could succeed in getting something of value from it, but instead only was able to get a few interesting thoughts. In the first place, the pedestrian statement that acoustic science has stim-

ulated musical production. Further, the acknowledgment of a parallel between Helmholtz and Ostwald in their negative attitude toward art seemed more or less on the mark. But this was not the allusion. Scientists often find art to be childish, but in this case, the position is inverted. . . . Very strange also this idea that the tempered chord is the work of science. I see in it only a practical aid, like the practical aid of the chemical industry's scale of colors. Of course we may use it for a bit, but we hardly have any need for a theory of colors. All the infinite mixtures possible will never produce a green Schweinfurt, a red Saturn, a violet cobalt. With us, a dark yellow is never mixed with black because it makes it green. Furthermore, the chemistry of colors passes blithely over all transparent mixtures (glazes). Not to mention their complete ignorance concerning the relativity of chromatic values. To hold that the possibility of creating harmony using a tone of equal value should become a general rule means renouncing the wealth of the soul. Thanks but no thanks.[5]

Instead, Klee elaborated a schematic drawing of his own ideas on colors, "the canon of totality" (figure 6). Above is light, below is darkness, and they are mutually interrelated (rather than distinct and separate, as in Kandinsky). In the middle of these, thanks to their relationship, gray is formed, around the axes of which, like the rings of Saturn, partially overlapping crescent-shaped wedges turn and blend. These indicate the three primary colors, blue, yellow, and red, which gradually become integrated functionally to produce the three intermediate colors, orange, green, and violet, thus recapitulating the

Colors and Color Theory

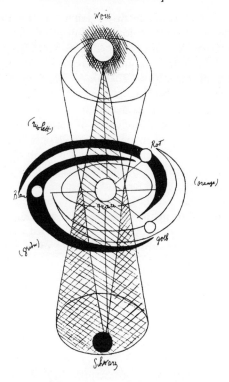

Weiss = white, *rot* = red, *gelb* = yellow, *schwarz* = black,
grün = green, *blau* = blue, *grau* = gray.

FIGURE 6

141

phenomenon of chromatic dispersion in the six-color circle, in which complementary colors stand in pairs (figure 7).

In this form, Kandinsky and Klee proposed from within the Bauhaus school the two most interesting thoughts on color, on which Johannes Itten (*The Art of Color*), Josef Albers (*Interaction of Color*), and Laszlo Moholy-Nagy (*Vision in Motion*) did little work. On the one hand, Itten returned to the original mystical-psychological concepts of essence and individual spirituality contained in physiognomic signs and chromatic expression, while on the other hand Moholy-Nagy considered the artificial mechanisms of perceptual psychology and certain automatic behaviors and pressures, despite the various distinctions (form, height, repetition, order) Albers made between physical form and psychological meaning. Here an intimate, nondialectical dualism is again confirmed: color as both sensation and substance, a dualism some languages still

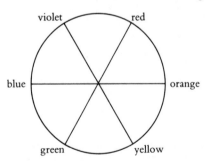

FIGURE 7

retain (as in the Russian *cvet*, color/perception, versus *kraska*, color/matter), verified in the commonplace laboratory of Kandinsky and Klee.

Kurt Koffka and Wolfgang Köhler, in Gestalt psychology, argued for those condensations of form and color in the vast realm of visual perception with expressly scientific intentions at the same time Klee was carrying out his program of color experimentation. The findings of Gestalt theory were broadened to the world of the arts (Rudolf Arnheim, *Art and Visual Perception*, 1954), but these thoughts on colors could only be seen in their relationship to Goethe's physiological and Kandinsky's spiritual theories. In turning away from those empirical schemas upon which the perceptual phenomena of human vision depended, the schemas could only be seen, in this chapter of the history of colors, as completely secondary, or certainly highly relative and inconsistent. Classical theories concerning sight similar to those of Gestalt psychology seem to be strictly "black-and-white" points of view, which manage to reach the world of color only in a circumspect way. Though considering the perceptual importance of colors, these theories assume the same posture that science manifested toward the arts: they see in it a childishness, which is as much as the arts will grant a stubborn, "meaningless" science in exchange. All the same, an attitude prevails that judges color as a product of form. This is exactly opposite to the fact of the primitive eye creating form in response to an immediate experience of color, which the spectacles of theoretical priorities would have us see only *after* the form. This question is, of course, related to the question of a psychology of form: one can determine by means of simple experiments the ages at which a child chooses on the basis of color and, only later, on the basis of form. Such a distinction between ages could occur only if *first* color is perceived and then form: the opposite of the theoretical sequence. This "truth of the form" thus results in the "color of the form" not as a meaning in itself but rather as the result of meanings, like that of ideas. Indeed, the schematic principles assumed by the arts tend to construct objects with colors that show the form, rather than the reverse, exalting in the game of their purity, so that the circle is red, the square is blue, the triangle yellow, and "whitewash" is praised (Le Corbusier).[6]

Nonetheless, the color theories proposed by Kandinsky, Klee, Itten, and Albers and independently by Sonia and Robert Delaunay were not developed apart from artistic work that served as a didactic and experimental workshop. As was the case for the operational proposals made by Chevreul or the successive systematic catalogues by A. H. Munsell, it was always a question of choices and comparisons with tones taken from nature, their production, and their similitude. This continued up to and including the recent theories on principles of composition and the historical birth of dye in the work of Faber Birren, the figurehead of color technology in modern America, where pragmatism, psychology, and history intersect on the subject of color.

In our century, an interest in establishing a system of colors was applied to colorimetry, based on the codification of metrological structures in the dye industry, or in tandem with experiments on the visual perception of colors (with inconclusive results). This is in fact the epitome of the modern history of color: colorimetric techniques and applied psychology, surveying and production.

Observations on Colors (1950) by Ludwig Wittgenstein, gathered together into a collection of aphorisms a few months before he died, appears despite the fragmentary nature of his considerations rather contrary to the experimentalism and "scientism" of Gestalt theories of perception, "which connect what seems with what is, while we can only speak of seeming, or connect what seems with what seems."

The point of departure here is, again, Goethe's *Farbenlehre*, in the interest in colors, which "stimulate philosophy . . . and seem to be resolved in an enigma that stimulates us—without making us anxious."

> God's essence would ensure his existence—which is to say, properly speaking, that it is not a case of existence.
>
> Can one not then also say that the essence of color ensures its existence? Contrary to what happens, let's say, with a white elephant. Which means in fact only that I cannot explain what "color" is, what the word "color" means, outside of a basis in a chromatic field. Thus, in this case, there is no explanation of "what colors *would be* if they *existed*."
>
> Now, it would be possible to state: one can describe how it would be if there were gods on Olympus—but not how it would be if God existed. And thereby, the concept "God" is more precisely defined.

How is it that we are taught the word "God" (or its use)? I cannot give in this regard an exhaustive grammatical description. However, I can, so to speak, offer contributions toward a description: I can say something about it, and perhaps, with time, add a sort of collection of examples.

Consider, in this regard, that a grammar book would freely give descriptions of how words were used but give a few examples or explanations. But consider also that to have more than that would not even be necessary. What would we do which such a long description? It would be useless if it were about the use of common words familiar to us already. But if we were to come up against a similar description of the use of a word in Assyrian? And in what language would it be useful? Certainly, in another that we spoke.—In the description often the word "sometimes" would appear, or "usually" or "almost always" or "almost never."

It is difficult to get a clear idea from this type of description.

And so, in the end, I am a painter, and often a very bad one.[7]

Here again we see how, through colors, every philosophical system finds itself shot through to the roots with uncertainty. Colors do not proceed from experiments but reside in concepts. In fact, simply taking them into consideration seems to create an internal incapacity to order them, since a science of colors, a natural history of colors, as it were, seems, in contrast to the life of animals, completely nonchronological. In logical operations and in speech, one needs to introduce propositions that one will "use," not just those one "thinks," following the thread of logic and empiricism.

It is impossible to produce clarity from deep darkness (Goethe): philosophical obscurity seems to be slightly shameful, and one must admit that logic must weave its way, like colors, between "affinity and opposition," putting what seems together with what seems, without confusing the semblance with reality, which may be but a semblance. These last ideas of Wittgenstein reflect an opposition to psychological and physiological theories in favor of logic, which ought to act as one expects a theory to function.

The appearance of white with respect to other colors constitutes a decisive difference, an "asymmetry of affinities" where the logical categories of transparency and cloudiness, lightness and darkness, appear as consequences of an original appearance (*Urphänomen*): an original phenomenon that is a preconceived idea and that takes hold of our eye and all of us. After space and time, colors are grouped in a region between two cultures, and if one is not interested in promulgating yet another theory of colors but rather "the logic of conceptions of color," one begins to see how such concepts must be dealt with according to the logical principles of transparency and opacity (this could be an ordering principle for the history of ideas itself).

Wittgenstein mentioned a new and thought-provoking proposal concerning the *Urphänomen* (once again, from Goethe) in which Freud recognized the simple dream of desires toward which—one can infer from the fragmentary quality of the

final aphorisms—impression and expression discover a ulte-
riori their point of application. Walter Benjamin discusses the
Urphänomen thus:

> Through the perception of colors, fantasy, as opposed
> to creative intuition, is preserved as an original phenom-
> enon (*Urphänomen*). Each form, indeed, each shape per-
> ceived by man corresponds to man's ability to produce
> it. The very body in dance, the hand in drawing imitate
> this shape and appropriate it. The limit of this capacity
> is still the world of color; the human body cannot create
> color. Its relation to it is not creative but rather recep-
> tive: the sparkle of color in one's eye. Even under the
> anthropologist's eye, sight is the watershed of the
> senses, since it simultaneously embraces form and color.
> And in such a moment it possesses on the one hand the
> capacity for active correspondence—perception of form
> and movement, hearing and voice—and on the other,
> however, the capacity for passive correspondence: the
> perception of color takes part in the sensory spheres of
> smell and taste. Language itself displays this unity in the
> group of words used—(*aus-*)*sehen, riechen, schmecken*—
> which refer as much to the object (transitive use) as to
> the human subject (intransitive use). In short: pure color
> is the instrument of fantasy, the land of dreams for a
> child lost in games, and not the rigid canon built by
> artists. This is connected to the "sensory-moral" action
> that Goethe intended in a patently romantic sense.
> "Transparent colors are limitless whether illuminated or
> in darkness, in the same way that fire and air can be
> understood as their highpoint and lowpoint. . . . The
> relationship between light and transparent color is infi-

nitely fascinating if one hazards an attempt to deepen it, and when colors catch fire, and mix, and reappear, and disappear, it is like breathing within the great spans of time between eternity and eternity, from the most exalted light to the eternal, solitary calm of the lowest gradations. Opaque colors, on the other hand, are like flowers that do not dare to reach for the sky and which, in any case, have more in common with weakness, with white, on the one hand, and with evil, with black, on the other. These latter, however, are quite capable of producing variations so sprightly and effects so natural that . . . the former, that is, transparent colors, in the end one comes to enjoy as spirits and are useful only to elevate the others." With these words, this "addition" from *Theory of Colors* does justify not only to the sensibility of those great colorists but also to the spirit of the very same childhood games. Think of all those games that appeal to the lively contemplation of fantasy: soap bubbles, tea parties, the color-filled evanescence of the magic lantern, drawing with crayons, imaginary friends. In all these cases, color weighs, light as the air, upon all things, for its charm comes not from the colored object or the pure, inanimate dye but, indeed, from its origin, its chromatic splendor and brilliance.[8]

Here it is a matter of a principle simulating truth, describing, beyond the full and empty spasms of positive and negative, dark and light, a new rationality that is, even for Wittgenstein, "the attitude of one who takes seriously a certain object but who then, at a certain, well determined *point*, no longer takes it seriously and declares something else to be more serious." There exist erroneous appearances that present themselves as real and others that have a confused, ephemeral character and that, as such, should be abandoned in the stream of logical judgment. This is no different from the certainty of the relative and the necessary in a passage from Lucretius: "Omnis enim color omnino mutatur in omnis (Every color changes completely in each thing)," like the fading color of purple that is lost thread by thread.[9]

As for the effect of substance and surface in color—its intensity, extension, and quality as the creative intellect behind intuition, as in Schopenhauer's *Sight and Colors* (1816 and 1854)—all this tends to disappear as an entirely intuitive piece of data, incorporated into a physiological environment and prefigured, normalized objects. In modern cities, one sees the appearance and disappearance of the material color of rusted metals and antioxidant paints, which take on the same reddish tones of the corrosive agent they are intended to fight (the Eiffel Tower, for example, or the metal scaffolding of Victorian train stations), or instead simulate as accurately as possible the sheen or grayness of soldered, shining metal. The contemporary industrial age seeks to display itself with the brilliance and shine of metal or with a covering of metallic colors: their garments appear as the lucid awareness of progress whose enamel is quickly stripped away by production. The specific research taking place concerning anticorrosive treatments for alloys (nickel plating, bronzing, nonrusting steel, anodized aluminum) tends, like a mechanical skin, to cover the body and the fate of objects, artificially

lengthening their lives under the sign of incorrupt-
ibility.

An "eternal color" appears everywhere in the brilliance and
glass clarity of varnishes and enamels, which give color the
startling effect of a "new" object, fresh from the factory. With
the near-exclusive use of shiny metal and plastic employed in
its place, one achieves in reality a falsification of the concept of
duration and the extermination of the more noble metals,
which, more than usury, evoke the sense of aging well and the
patina of time: copper, brass, bronze, lead. And we are speaking not of a wider use of true metals but rather the spread of
shiny metal surfaces as "colors" that take on the aspect of
polished glass, completely overtaking the color prestige of
other metals, which then appear simply as decorative or artistic details.

Alongside this aesthetic of "shine" moving between object
and product, the body of the modern city takes on a tonality
within the range of gray, not simply due to the process of
obfuscation and soiling accelerated nowadays from the dust
and pollution of industry and traffic, but also because of the
colorless construction materials being used, like asphalt or
cement, in marked contrast to the tonalities of the nineteenth-
century cities still visible today.[10] The washing and bleaching
of historic buildings and facades looking onto city streets in
order to recover a truer color has attempted to remove the
layers of dust to reveal the clearer tones of artistic details, but
only till they are once again covered with a new layer of city
black. The absence of color from metropolitan buildings dur-

ing the day can be perfectly captured in black-and-white photography and is in marked contrast to its nighttime
appearance, made up of multicolored flashing lights and
ephemeral furnishings.

Finally, interior objects and furnishings have undergone a
gamut of shades, unnatural colors, not without harmony but
rather artificially harmonized to reflect their colorless space on
the faces of those who live with them. The white of domestic
appliances and bathroom furnishings represents the imposition of old visual norms concerning hygiene, but once imposed, the objective is more easily extended to personal
clothing in more "pleasing" shades. Other, similar products
in the marketplace of furnishings and clothing propose, unmistakably, the shades of navy blue or light brown as the
intermediaries of gray, even while the isolated, postmodern
explosions of color call forth a countermovement of even
more tenacious neutrality. Within this tired atmosphere,
which flattens imagination and recognition, the coloring of
food and drink carry out a further process of denaturation of
the product through external treatments that make use of color
through an artificial esthetic that, we discover, actually en-
dangers our health: colors are poisons.

The dominant gray of the modern city appears yet again in
the casual mixtures and manifestations of those atonal colors
(red, yellow, blue) that are called primary but that no painter
would ever use. These disappear in the very moment in which
they are employed as the visual stimuli of signs or for inexpressive, indistinguishable markers. This gray, while perhaps

not completely inert but smothering all individuation in hundreds of tones—such is the modern eye—nevertheless finds itself juxtaposed to green, a color absolutely vital to the hopes of our civilization and to its promise that it not be the last in nature. The morality of green for everyone, a color as much as a right that should be denied to no one, but that is continuously taken away with the promise of even greater frontiers, takes on the fluctuating organic nature, both present and removed, of the color of blood, to which is added, as to green, the soot of curdled, scorched garbage. Here are the remains of the tragic game between "functional" colors and "natural" colors, in which both prove toxic.

From this point, writes Kandinsky, "gray is void of resonance and immobile. This immobility, however, is of a different nature than the tranquillity of green, which is located between two active colors and is their product. Gray is thus an inconsolable immobility. The darker gray makes things, the greater the inconsolability and suffocating oppression. If instead one is given in the light a kind of air, the potential for breathing, one can enter into the color itself which contains with a certain element of hidden hope."[11] This hope ought not to be contradicted by saving nature through gray. An abstract painter who had, for the sake of color, renounced the rest of painting, the day before his suicide painted one last picture, completely gray, with only a few small flames of yellow.

With colors we have described a charming and tragic play of events. Perhaps this story will enable us to learn from our past.

NOTES

CHAPTER 1. SENSE AND BODY IN COLORS

1. Isaac Newton, *Optiks: or, a Treatise on the Reflections, Refractions, Inflections and Colours of Light*, 4th ed. (London; Innys, 1730). Newton's color wheel is discussed on pp. 154–58.

2. This schema is taken from Brent Berlin and Paul Kay, *Basic Color Terms* (Berkeley and Los Angeles, 1969).

3. See Eugène Chevreul, *Cercles chromatiques . . . réproduit au moyen de la chromocalcographie* (Paris, 1855), and the tables in the *Atlas* of this author's major work, *De la loi du contraste simultané des couleurs . . .* (Paris, 1839).

CHAPTER 2. COLOR AS FIGURE AND FATE

1. Quoted in Paolo Rovesti, *Alla ricerca dei cosmetici perduti* (Venice: Marsilio, 1975), p. 38.

2. Claude Levi-Strauss, *Tristi tropici* (Milan: Saggiatore, 1975), pp. 179–80.

3. Mario Equicola, *Libro de natura de amore* (Book on the nature of love) (Venice, 1525), fol. 183r–v.

4. Friedrich Nietzsche, *Daybreak: Thoughts on the Prejudices of Morality*, trans. R. J. Hollingdale (Cambridge: Cambridge University Press, 1982), p. 182.

5. See Robert Graves, *I Miti greci* (*Greek Myths*) (Milan: Longanesi, 1955), 69, 112, 583, 744, 805. Eros is said to be the son of Iris and the West Wind; he takes on the function of Iris as messenger of the Gods (Zeus, Hera, et al.); his belt serves as a leash for the lion Nemeus.

Notes

6. Virgil, *Aeneid*, 9:349–50: "purpuream vomit ille animam et cum sanguine mixta / vina refert moriens, hic furto fervidus instat,"; and *Georgics*, 4:372–73: "Eridanus, quo non alius per pinguia culta / in mare purpureum violentior effluit amnis."

7. Procopius, *Secret History*, trans. Richard Atwater (Ann Arbor: University of Michigan Press, 1961), pp. 35–40.

8. A useful summary of Shiite cosmological symbolism can be found in Mohammed Karim-Khan Kermani, *The Book of the Red Hyacinth* (1851), in which there is no lack of references to the westernized Arab tradition concerning the ideas of Alhazen (Abu Ali al-Hasan ibn al-Haytham) on perspective and optics. Those ideas find a correspondence in the post-Goethian theosophy of Rudolf Steiner, who himself drew from the pre-Islamic Persian religions (Mazdaism). Kermani's colors, distinguished by their "existence" and their "manifestation," are gathered into a symbolic order that is not abstract but rather is based on an "integral spiritual realism": light is the spirituality of color, and color is the corporeal element of light; in other words, the spirit is "light in fusion," and the body is "solidified light." This theme can also be found in all platonic and idealist philosophy.

Primordial colors linked to the natural elements of fire, air, water, and earth (note the analogies to Western natural scientists such as Paracelsus, Bernardino Telesio, Giordano Bruno, Geronimo Cardano, and Giambattista della Porta) are, according to Shiite doctrine, white, yellow, red, and black respectively. These retain connections to the principles of heat (masculine) and cold (feminine), though the correspondence between elements and senses is given as follows: Fire and color, Air and sound, Water and smell, Earth and taste.

The "subtle body" of colors cannot be seen with the eye, but participates in a purer level of existence and an extreme level of intensity. In this sense, in terms of their "imaginific" nature, intelligence is white, spirit is yellow, soul is green, nature is red, matter is ashen gray, imagination is bright green, and body is black (cf. Henry Corbin, *Temple et contemplation* [Paris: Flammarion, 1980]). Among the subtle colors blue does not in fact appear; though materially quite common in Islamic practice, it is actually

a part of Christian spirituality, in particular a symbol of the body/soul
conflict at the basis of that spirituality.

9. Cennino Cennini, *Il libro dell'arte* (The book of art), ed. Franco
Brunello (Venice: Neri Pozza, 1971), pp. 64–65.

10. Marco Polo, *Il milione* (The million), ed. Danielle Ponchiroli
(Turin: Einaudi, 1954), chapter 35, "On Baloscan (Badasian [Badahk-
shan]," p. 40.

CHAPTER 3. COLORS AND FORM

1. Ludovico Antonio Muratori, *Antiquitates italicae medii aevi* (Milan,
1738–43), 2:364–87.

2. *De coloribus et artibus romanorum*, ed. A. Giry (Paris, 1873);
A. Ilg, *Heraclius: De coloribus et artibus romanorum* (Vienna, 1873).

3. Tommaso Campanella, *Opere* (Works), ed. R. Amerio (Milan:
Ricciardi, 1956), "Sopra i colori delle vesti" (On the color of clothing),
p. 852.

4. See chapter 7, n. 4.

CHAPTER 4. COLOR IN DRAWING AND PAINTING

1. Aristotle, *Poetics* (1450): 1–3.

2. Lorenzo Valla, *Epistula ad candidum decembrum* in *opera* (Basel,
1540), pp. 639–41. Cf. Michael Baxandall, *Painting and Experience in Fifteenth Century Italy* (Oxford, 1972).

3. Carlo Pedretti, *Leonardo da Vinci on Painting: A Lost Book* (Berkeley
and Los Angeles, 1964), p. 57; also in *Scritti d'arte del Cinquecento* (Writings on the art of the sixteenth century), vol. 9, *Colore*, ed. P. Barocchi
(Turin: Einaudi, 1979), p. 2144. Leonardo's experiment with stained glass
anticipates the hypothesis on additive and subtractive colors.

4. Eugène Delacroix, *Oeuvres littéraires* (Paris, 1923), pp. 71–74.

Notes

5. *Antonii Thylesii consentini de coloribus libellus, in Actuarii Joannis Zacchariae filii . . . ,* book 7, "De urinis," (Paris 1548), to which is added *Aristotelis stagiritae de coloribus, a Coelio Calcagnino interprete.* The first edition of Antonioi Telesio is the 1528 Venice edition, given in its entirety in Johann Wolfgang von Goethe, *Materialien zur Geschichte der Farbenlehre* (Materials for a history of color theory) (Tübingen: Cotta, 1810); rpt., *Geschichte der Farbenlehre,* 2 vols. (Munich: DTV, 1971).

6. Paolo Pino, *Dialogo di pittura* (A dialogue on painting) (Venice, 1548), ed. C. Camesasca (Milan: Rizzoli, 1954), pp. 46–47.

7. The complete title is *Dialogue on the painting of M. Ludovico Dolce, entitled the Aretino, in which the dignity of this painting is discussed along with the necessary elements a perfect painter must possess. With examples of ancient and modern painters; and at the end mention is made of the virtues and works of the divine Titian* (Venice, 1557).

8. Giorgio Vasari, *Lives of Seventy of the Most Eminent Painters, Sculptors, and Architects,* ed. E. H. Blashfield, E. W. Blashfield, and A. A. Hopkins (New York: Charles Scribner's Sons, 1911), 3:2–3.

9. Roger de Piles, *La bilancia dei pittori* (The scale of painters), in Elizabeth G. Holt, *A Documentary History of Art* (New York, 1957–58). Absolute perfection in painting is divided into twenty degrees or parts, a complete classification of which we proposed with the following table.

Names of Famous Painters	Composition	Drawing	Color	Expression
Albani	14	14	10	6
Albrecht Dürer	8	10	10	8
Andrea del Sarto	12	16	9	8
Barocci	14	15	6	10
Bassano Jacopo	6	8	17	0
(Se)bastiano del Piombo	8	13	16	7
Bellini Giovanni	4	6	14	0
Bourdon	10	8	8	4
LeBrun	16	16	8	16
P. Caliari Veronese	15	10	16	3
I Carracci	15	17	13	13

Notes

Names of Famous Painters	Composition	Drawing	Color	Expression
Correggio	13	13	15	12
Dan. da Volterra	12	15	5	8
Diepenbeck	11	10	14	6
Il Domenichino	15	17	9	17
Giorgione	8	9	18	4
Giovanni da Udine	10	8	16	3
Giulio Romano	15	16	4	14
Il Guercino	18	10	10	4
Il Guido (Reni)	–	13	9	12
Holbein	9	10	16	3
Jac. Jordaens	10	8	16	6
Luc. Jordaens	13	12	9	6
Josepin (Gius. d'Arpino)	10	10	6	2
Lanfranco	14	13	10	5
Leonardo da Vinci	15	16	4	14
Lucas van Leyden	8	6	6	4
Michaelangelo Buonarroti	8	17	4	8
Michaelangelo Caravaggio	6	6	16	0
Murillo	6	8	15	4
Otho Venius (Oct. van Veen)	13	14	10	10
Palma Il Vecchio	5	6	16	0
Palma Il Giovane	12	9	14	6
Il Parmigianino	10	15	6	6
Fr. Penni, il Fattore	0	15	8	0
Perino del Vaga	15	16	7	6
Pietro da Cortona	16	14	12	6
Pietro Perugino	4	12	10	4
Polidoro da Caravaggio	10	17	–	15
Pordenone	8	14	17	5
Pourbus	4	15	6	6
Poussin	15	17	6	15
Primaticcio	15	14	7	10
Raphael	17	18	12	18
Rembrandt	15	6	17	12
Rubens	18	13	17	17

Names of Famous Painters	Composition	Drawing	Color	Expression
Fr. Salviati	13	15	8	8
Le Sueur	15	15	4	15
Teniers	15	12	13	6
Pietro Testa	11	15	0	6
Tintoretto	15	14	16	4
Titian	12	15	18	6
Van Dyck	15	10	17	13
Vanius	15	15	12	13
Taddeo Zuccaro	13	14	10	9
Federico Zuccaro	10	13	8	8

10. Galileo Galilei, *Il saggiatore* (The Essayist), ed. Ferdinando Flora (Turin, 1977), pp. 223–24.

11. Goethe, *Geschichte der Farbenlehre*, 1:167.

CHAPTER 5. COLOR AND ITS ORDER

1. Voltaire, *Philosophical Letters* (1733), trans. Ernest Dilworth (Indianapolis: Bobbs-Merrill, 1961), pp. 76–77.

2. Friedrich Hegel, *Estetica*, ed. N. Merker (Turin: Einaudi, 1967), p. 161.

3. Harald Küppers, *La couleur: Origine, méthodologie, application* (Paris: Office du Livre, 1975). For a complete discussion of chromatic solids, see Attilio Marcolli, *Teoria del campo* (Theory of field) (Florence: Sansoni, 1978), 2:377–401.

CHAPTER 6. ACTION COLORS AND PASSION COLORS

1. Johann Wolfgang von Goethe, *Campagne in Frankreich* (1792), Italian trans. *Incomincia la novella storia* (A new history begins) (Palermo: Sellerio, 1981), pp. 29–30.

2. Friedrich Hegel, *Aforismi ienensi* (Milano: Fetrinelli, 1981), p. 58. On the subject of shadows, see Jean-Henri Hassenfratz, *Observations sur les ombres colorées* (Paris, 1872).

Notes

3. Johann Wolfgang von Goethe, *Theory of Colors*, trans. Charles Lock Eastlake (London: John Murray, 1840), from the chapter "Effect of Color with Reference to Moral Associations."

4. Francesco Algarotti, *Saggio sopra la pittura* (Essay on painting), ed. G. da Pozzo, (Bari: Laterza, 1963), p. 81.

5. Gottfried Semper, "The Origin of Polychromy in Architecture," in James Owen, *An Apology for the Colouring of the Greek Court* (London: Bradbury & Evans, 1854), pp. 47–56.

CHAPTER 7. THE COLOR OF COLOR

1. [Jean-Baptiste Colbert], *Instruction générale pour la teinture des laines et manufactures de la laine de toutes couleurs, et pour la culture des drogues ou ingrédiens qu'on y employe* (Paris: Muguey, 1671).

2. E. Fiorani and F. Vidoni, eds., *Il giovane Engels: Cultura, classe e materialismo dialettico* (The young Engels: Culture, class, and dialectical materialism) (Milan: Mazzotta, 1974), p. 243.

3. Herman Melville, *Moby Dick*, chapter 42.

4. Gasparo Gozzi, *L'osservatore veneto* (The Venetian observer), ed. N. Raffaelli (Milan: Rizzoli, 2: 304–5. The letter is dated June 1762.

5. Rimbaud himself explicates his famous "Sonnet des Voyelles" (Sonnet of vowels) in "Alchimia del verbo" (Alchemy of the word), in *Illuminations* (Paris, 1886): "I have invented the color of the vowels! A black, E white, I red, O blue, U green. I have codified the form and movement of each consonant and, through instinctive rhythms, I am proud to have invented a poetry accessible, one day or another, to all the senses. I shall keep the translation to myself."

CHAPTER 8. COLORS AND COLOR THEORY

1. Louis Ducos du Hauron, *Les couleurs en photographie: Solution du problème* (Colors in photography: A solution to the problem) (Paris: Marion, 1869), p. 5.

Notes

2. The function of color in neoplastic architecture is stated by Theo van Doesburg (1925), in Francesco La Regina, *Architettura, storia e politica* (Architecture, history, and politics) (Bari: De Donato, 1976), pp. 165–66. "The new architecture has suppressed the individual expression of painting, the painting itself, an expression of harmony through imagination and illusion indirectly using naturalistic forms, or more directly, built up by planes of various colors. The new architecture uses color organically by itself. Color is one of the elementary means for making visible the harmony of architectonic relationships. Without color, these proportional relations would not take on a living reality of their own, and it is through color that architecture becomes the end of all plastic research in space and time. In a neutral, achromatic architecture, the equilibrium of relations between architectonic elements is invisible. For this reason a final note is sought: a painting (on a wall) or a sculpture in a space. But there has always been a dualism that goes back to the era when real life and the life of beauty were separate from each other. The suppression of this dualism has long been the mission of all artists. When modern architecture was born, the painter-builder found his true creative field. He organizes color aesthetically in time-space and makes plastically visible a new dimension."

3. See Goethe, *Geschichte der Farbenlehre*, 2:148–49, where he summarizes Hoffmann's linguistic, chromatic-musical synthesis. Note how there is no corresponding term for *Schlatten* (shadow): "Licht/Laut, Dunkelheit/Schwigen; Schatten; Lichtstrahlen/Schallstahlen; Farbe/Ton; Farbenkorper/Instrument; Ganze Farben/Ganze Tone; Gemischte Farben/Halbe Tone; Gebrochenem Farbe/Abweichung des Tones; Helle/Hohe; Dunkel/Tiefe; Farbenreihe/Oktave; Wiederholte Farbenreihe/Mehere Oktaven; Helldunkel/Unisono; Himmlische Farben/Hohe Tone; Irdische (braune) Farben/Kontratone; Herrschender Ton/Solostimme; Licht und Halbschatten/Prime und Sekundstimme."

4. Franz Marc, *I cento aforismi: La seconda vita* (A hundred aphorisms: The second life), ed. Renato Troncon, with an essay by Giorgio Franck (Milan: Feltrinelli, 1982), pp. 66–67.

5. See Placido Cherchi, *Paul Klee teorico* (Paul Klee, theoretician) (Bari: De Donato, 1978), pp. 160–161.

Notes

6. The spontaneous association of the three colors to the three elementary geometric figures came about somewhat differently in the experience of the Bauhaus and was a way to establish the attitudes of their pupils: yellow-triangle, red-square, blue-circle, and in the same way with the pyramid, cube, and sphere. In 1931, Le Corbusier developed, all the same, a program of shades for interiors to be applied like wallpaper and titled in concordance with the classic themes of the avant-garde *claviers des couleurs* (keyboard of colors). These unusual chromatic groupings were classified according to "the quality of their mural significance"—"space," "sky," "velvet," "wall," and "sand"—and were offered to designers and architects with the commercialized product Salubra; see Luisa Martina Colli, "Le Corbusier e il colore: I claviers Salubra" (Le Corbusier and color: The Salubra keyboards), in *Storia dell'arte* 43, (1981): 272–93.

7. Ludwig Wittgenstein, *Pensieri diversi* (Various thoughts) (Milan: Adelphi, 1980), pp. 150–51. Also idem, *Osservazioni sui colori* (Observations on colors), ed. R. Trinchero (Turin: Einaudi, 1981), *passim* for the above quote.

8. Walter Benjamin, "Sbirciando nel libro per bambini" (Poring over children's books) (1926), in *Orbis pictus: Scritti sulla letteratura infantile* (The world of pictures: Writings on children's literature), ed. Giulio Schiavoni (Milano: Emme, 1981), pp. 57–58.

9. Titus Lucretius Carus, *De rerum natura*, vv. 749–841, where he speaks broadly about color.

10. See the chromatic tables summarizing colors used in cities in Giovanni Brino and Franco Rosso, *Colore e citta: Il piano del colore di Torino, 1800–1850* (Color and city: The color plan of Turin, 1800–1850) (Turin: Idea, 1980).

11. Wassily Kandisky, *Lo spirituale nell'arte* (On the spiritual in art) (Bari: De Donato, 1972), p. 69.

BIBLIOGRAPHY

Adrosko, Rita J. "Natural Dyes in the United States." *National Museum Bulletin* no. 281 (1968).

———. *Natural Dyes and Home Dyeing.* New York, 1971.

Albers, Josef. *Interaction of Color.* New Haven, Conn., 1963. Reprint. Westford, Mass., 1980.

Alberti, Leon Battista. *Della pittura* (1436). Edited by L. Mallé. Florence, 1950.

Albrecht, H. J. *Farbe als Sprache.* Cologne, 1974.

Algarotti, Francesco. *Il neutonianismo ovvero dialoghi sopra la luce, i colori e la attrazione* (1737), 6th ed. Naples, 1746

[Aristotle]. *Aristotelis stagiritae de coloribus a Coelio Calcagnino interprete.* In Joannes Actuaris, *De urinis.* Paris, 1548.

———. *De coloribus libellus Aristotelis a Simone Portio interprete latinitate donatus et commentariis illustratus.* Florence, 1548.

Armenini, Giovan Battista. *De' veri precetti della pittura . . . libri III.* Ravenna, 1586.

Arnheim, Rudolf. *Art and Visual Perception.* Berkeley Calif., 1954.

Bancroft, Edward. *Experimental Researches Concerning the Philosophy of Permanent Colours.* 2 vols. London, 1794. Reprint. Philadelphia, 1814.

Barocchi, P., ed. *Scritti d'arte del Cinquecento.* Vol. 9. *Colore.* Turin, 1979.

Berlin, Brent, and Paul Kay. *Basic Color Terms.* Berkeley and Los Angeles, 1969.

Bezold, Wilhelm von. *Die Farbenlehre im Hinblick auf Kunst und Kunstgewerbe.* Brunswick, 1874.

Birren, Faber. *Creative Color.* New York, 1961.

———. *Color: A Survey in Words and Pictures.* New York, 1963.

———. *Light, Color, and Environment: A Thorough Presentation of Facts on the Biological and Psychological Effects of Color.* New York, 1969.

Bibliography

Boyle, Robert. *Experiments and Considerations Touching Colours*. London, 1664.

Brino, Giovanni, and Franco Rosso. *Colore e città: Il piano del colore di Torino, 1800–1850*. Milan, 1980.

Brunello, Franco. *L'arte della tintura nella storia dell'umanità*. Venice, 1968.

———, ed. *De arte illuminandi*. Venice, 1975.

Brusatin, Manlio, "Colore." In *Enciclopedia*, vol. 3, *Città–Cosmologie*, pp. 388–411. Turin, 1978.

Burano, Giochino [Giovanni Barich]. *Trattato sopra l'arte della tintura*. Venice, 1794.

Cardano, Gerolamo. *Opere omnia*. 10 vols. Lyons, 1663. Vol. 2, chapter 10, "De gemmis et coloribus."

Castel, Louis-Bernard. *L'optique des couleurs, fondée sur les simples observations et tournée surtout à la pratique de la peinture, de la teinture et des autres arts coloristes*. Paris, 1740.

Cennini, Cennino. *Il libro dell'arte* (1437). Edited by F. Brunello. Venice, 1968.

Chevreul, Eugène. "Atlas." In *Del la loi du contraste simultané des couleurs et de l'assortiment des objets colorés, considérés d'après cette loi dans ses rapports avec la peinture, les tapisseries. . . .* Paris, 1839.

———. *Recherches expérimentales sur la peinture à l'huile. . . .* n.p., [*1850*].

———. "Atlas." In *Exposé d'un moyen de définir et nommer les couleurs, d'après une méthode précise et expérimentale. . . .* Paris, 1861.

———. *Des couleurs et de leurs applications aux arts industriels, à l'aide des cercles chromatiques. . . .* Paris, 1864.

———. *Des arts qui parlent aux yeux au moyen de solides colorés d'une étendue sensible, et en particulier des arts du tapissier des Gobelins. . . .* Paris, 1867.

———. *De la différence et de l'analogie de la méthode a posteriori expérimentale, dans ses applications aux sciences du concret et aux sciences morales et politiques*. Paris, [*1870*].

Clerk-Maxwell, James. "On the Theory of Colours in Relation to Colour-Blindness." In *Researches on Colour-Blindness*, edited by George Wilson. Edinburgh, 1855.

[Colbert, Jean-Baptiste]. *Instruction générale pour la teinture des laines et manufactures de la laine de toutes couleurs, et pour la culture des drogues ou ingrédiens qu'on y employe.* Paris, 1671.

Colore. Milan: Marshall Editions, 1982.

Delacroix, Eugène. *Oeuvres littéraires.* Paris, 1923.

Delaunay, Sonia, and Robert Delaunay. *The New Art of Color.* New York, 1978.

Déribéré, Maurice. *La couleur.* Paris, 1964.

———. *La couleur dans la publicité et la vente.* Paris, 1969.

Dolce, M. Lodovico. *Dialogo . . . nel quale si ragiona della qualità, diversità e proprietà de i colori.* Venice, 1565.

Ducos de Hauron, Louis. *Les couleurs en photographie: Solution du problème.* Paris, 1869.

———. *La triplice photographie des couleurs et l'imprimerie, système de photochromographie. . . .* Paris, 1897.

Duplessis, Yvonne. *La vision parapsychologique des couleurs.* Paris, 1974.

Eisenstein, Sergey M. *Izbrannye prorzvedenija v šesti tomach.* Moscow, 1963–70. Vol. 3. *Cvet.*

Faivre, E. *Oeuvres scientifiques de Goethe, analysées et appréciées.* Paris, 1862.

Fraunhofer, Joseph. *Beistimmung des Brechungs- und Farbenzerstreuungsvermögens verschiedener Glasarten in Bezug auf die Vervollkommnung achromatischer Fernröhre. . . .* Leipzig, 1905.

Frieling, H. *Mensch, Farbe, Raum,* 2d ed. Munich, 1956.

———. *Farbe in Raum.* Munich, 1974.

———. *Mensch und Farbe.* Munich, 1977.

Gladstone, William Ewart. *Studies on Homer and the Homeric Age.* Oxford, 1858.

Goethe, Johann Wolfgang von. *[Materialien zur] Geschichte der Farbenlehre.* 2 vols. 1810. 2d ed. Munich, 1971.

———. *Erklärung der Tafeln: Anzeige und Übersicht* [Tübingen, 1810].

———. *Zur Farbenlehre.* 2 vols. Tübingen, 1810. *Theory of Colors.* Translated by Charles Lock Eastlake. London, 1840.

Gregory, R. L. *Eye and Brain: Psychology of Seeing.* Cambridge, 1966.

Guaita, L. *La scienza dei colori e la pittura.* Milan, 1893.

Guerrini, O., and C. Ricci, eds. *Il libro de i colori: Segreti del secolo XV.* Bologna, 1887.

Bibliography

Guillerme, Jacques. *Lumière et couleur*. Monte Carlo, 1960.

————. *L'atelier du temps*. Paris, 1964.

Hay, D. R. *The Laws of Harmonious Colouring, Adapted to Interior Decorations*. 6th ed. London, 1847.

Hedfords, H., ed. *Compositiones ad tingenda musiva* (8th century). Uppsala, Sweden, 1932.

Helmholtz, H. von. *Handbuch der physiologischen Optik*. Leipzig, 1867.

Hendrie, R. *An Essay upon Various Arts by Theophilus, Called Also Rugerus*. London, 1847.

Henzel, Johann. "Relativitätstheorie und Ostwald's Farbenlehre in der Leipziger Zentenorfeiner." *Neuer Winterthurer Taghlott* nos. 285–90 (1922).

Higgins, S. H. *History of Bleaching*. London, 1924.

Home, F. *Experiments on Bleaching*. Edinburgh, 1756.

Ilg, A. *Heraclius: De coloribus et artibus romanorum*. Vienna, 1873.

Itten, Johannes. *Kunst der Farbe*. Ravensburg, Germany, 1961. *The Art of Color*. New York, 1974.

Jodin, A. *Étude comparative sur les noms des couleurs*. Paris, 1903.

Kalmus, H. *Diagnosis and Genetics of Defective Colour Vision*. Oxford, 1965.

Kandinsky, Wassily. *Über Geistige in der Kunst*. Munich, 1912. *Concerning the Spiritual in Art*. Translated by M. T. Sadler. Mineola, N.Y., 1977.

Katz, David, *The World of Colour*. London, 1935.

————. *Gestalt Psychology*. New York, 1950.

Kepes, Gyorgy. *Language of Vision*. Chicago, 1945.

Kircher, Athanasius. *Ars magna lucis et umbrae*. Rome, 1646.

Klee, Paul. *Teoria della forma e della figurazione*. 2 vols. Basel, 1956. 3d ed. Milan, 1976.

Küppers, Harald. *La couleur: Origine, méthodologie, application*. Paris, 1975.

————. *Farben Atlas*. Cologne, 1978.

Land, E. H. "Experiments in Color Vision." *Scientific American* (May, 1959).

Lassaigne, I. L. *Dizionario pittoresco e cromascopio dei reagenti chimici*. 2 vols. Mantua, 1840.

Bibliography

Laurie, Arthur P. *The Pigments and Mediums of the Great Painters*. London, 1949.

————. *The Painter's Methods and Materials*. New York, 1967.

Lecoy de la Marche, Albert. *L'art d'enluminer*. Paris, 1980.

McAdam, D. L., ed. *Sources of Color Science*. Cambridge, 1970.

Magnus, H. F. *Die geschichtliche Entwicklung des Farbensinnes*. Leipzig, 1877.

Malevich, Kazimir. *La lumière et la couleur*. Lausanne, Switzerland, 1981.

[Marat, Jean-Paul]. *Notions élémentaires d'optique*. Paris, 1784.

Marcolli, Attilio. *Teoria del campo*. Vol. 2. *Corso di metodologia della visione*. Florence, 1978.

Marsilli, Luigi Ferdinando. *Annotazione intorno alla grana de' tintori della kermes.* . . . Venice, 1711.

Marx, Ellen. *Les contrastes de la couleur*. Paris, 1973.

Matthaei, Rupprecht. *Goethe's Color Theory*. New York, 1971.

Mauthner, Ludwig. *Farbenlehre.* . . . Wiesbaden, Germany, 1894.

Merrifield, Mary P. *A Treatise on Painting Written by Cennino Cennini in the Year 1437*. London, 1844.

Maholy-Nagy, Laszlo. *Vision in Motion*. Chicago, 1947.

Morato, Fulvio Pellegrino. *Del significato de' colori e de' mazzolli* (1535). Venice, 1564.

Munsell, A. H. *A Color Notation*. Boston, 1913.

Newton, Isaac. *Optiks; or, A Treatise on Reflections, Refractions, Inflections, and Colours of Light*. 4th ed. London, 1730.

Ostwald, Wilhelm. *Beiträge zur Farbenlehre*. Leipzig, 1917.

————. *Goethe, Schopenhauer und die Farbenlehre*. Leipzig, 1918.

————. *Die Farbenlehre*. 4 vols. 1919, 2d ed. Leipzig, 1922.

Parrish, Charles Henry. *The Significance of Color in the Negro Community*. Chicago, n.d.

Parson, J. Herbert. *An Introduction to the Study of Colour Vision*. Cambridge, 1915.

Perret, August. *Couleurs minérales*. Paris 1902.

Perspach, H. *La mosaïque*. Paris, [1889].

Petersen, P. *Goethe und Aristoteles*. Berlin, 1919.

Bibliography

Pfeiffer, Henri. *L'harmonie des couleurs.* 4th ed. Paris, 1972.

Piazza, Bartolomeo. *L'iride sagra spiegata ne i colori degli abiti ecclesiastici.* Rome, 1682.

Piles, Roger de. *Recueil de divers ouvrages sur le peinture et le coloris.* Paris, 1755.

Pileur d'Apligny, Placide-Auguste le. *Traité des couleurs matérielles et de la manière de colorer. . . .* Paris, 1779. Reprint. Geneva, 1973.

Pino, Paolo. *Dialogo di pittura* (1548). Edited by C. Camesasca. Milan, 1954.

Pomet, Pierre. *Histoire générale des drogues. . . .* Paris, 1694.

Portal, P.-P.-F. de. *Des couleurs symboliques dans l'antiquité, le moyen âge et les temps modernes.* Paris, 1837. Reprint. 1975.

Previati, Gaetano. *I principi scientifici del divisionismo.* Turin, 1929.

Rebora, Giovanni. *Un manuale di tintoria del Quattrocento.* Milan, 1970.

Ricciardi, Achille. *Il teatro del colore: Estetica del dopoguerra.* Milan, 1920.

Richter, Jean Paul. *The Notebooks of Leonardo da Vinci.* 2 vols. London, 1883. Reprint. New York, 1970.

Richter, Manfred. *Internationale Bibliographie der Farbenlehre und ihrer Grenzgebiete.* Göttingen, Germany. 1952.

Rinaldi, Giovanni de'. *Il mostruosissimo mostro di G. de' R.: Nel primo de' quali si ragiona del significato de' colori: Nel secondo si tratta dell'herbe, e fiori.* Venice, 1599.

Rizzetti, Giovanni. *De luminis affectionibus: Specimen phisico-mathematicum.* Bergamo, Italy, 1727.

Rochas, Albert de. *L'extériorisation de la sensibilité: Étude expérimentale et historique.* 2d ed. Paris, 1895.

Roesler, R. *Zur Etymologie der Farbenbezeichnungen auf dem romanischer Sprachgebiete.* Vienna, 1868.

Rood, Ogden N. *Modern Chromatics.* New York, 1879.

Rosa, Michele. *Dissertazione della porpora e della materia vestiaria presso gli antichi.* Modena, 1786.

Rosetti, Giovanventura. *Plichto de larte de tentori che insegna a tenger pani telle banbasi et sede si per larthe mahiore come per la comune.* Venice, 1540.

———. *Notandissimi secreti de l'arte profumatoria* (Venice, 1555). Edited by F. Brunello and F. Facchetti. Venice, 1973.

Bibliography

Rüscher, M. de. *Histoire naturelle de la cochinelle pietrifiée par des documents autentiques.* Amsterdam, 1729.

Sahlins, Marshall. "Colori e cultura." *Rassegna italiana di sociologia* 4 (1975).

Schlechta, K. *Goethe in seinem Verhältnis zu Aristoteles.* Frankfurt, 1938.

Schopenhauer, Arthur. *Sämmtliche Werke.* Edited by J. Frauenstadt. Vol. I, part 2. "Über das Sehn und die Farben." Part 3. "Theoria colorum physiologica." Leipzig, 1877.

Schott, Caspar. *Technica curiosa sive mirabilia artis.* 2 vols. Nuremburg, 1664.

Schütznberger, Paul. *Traité des matières colorantes comprenant leurs applications à la teinture et à l'impression.* . . . 2 vols. Paris, 1867.

Semper, Gottfried. "The Origin of Polychromy in Architecture." In J. Owen, *An Apology for the Colouring of the Greek Court.* London, 1854.

———. *Der Stil in den technischen und tektonischen Künsten: Ein Handbuch oder praktischen Aestetik, für Techniker, Künstler und Kunstfreunde.* . . . 2 vols. Frankfurt, 1860–63.

Signac, Paul. *D'Eugène Delacroix au Neo-Impressionisme.* 2d ed. Paris, 1921.

Steiner, Rudolf. *Über das Wesen der Farben.* Stuttgart, 1959. *Colour.* London, 1982.

Talier, Angelo Natale. *Dell 'arte di tingere . . . opera ricavata dai più celebri recenti autori inglesi e francesi.* . . . Venice, 1793.

Tallier, Gallipedo. *Nuovo plico d'ogni sorte di tinture, arricchito di vari e bellissimi segreti per colorire animale, vegetale e minerali.* Venice, 1704.

Teevan, R. C., and R. C. Birney. *Colour Vision.* New York, 1961.

Telesio, Antonio. *De coloribus.* . . . Venice, 1528, 2d ed. Paris, 1548.

Telesio, Bernardini. *De colorum generatione opusculum.* Naples, 1570.

Teyssèdre, Bernard. *Roger de Piles et les débats sur les couleurs au siècle de Louis XIV.* . . . Paris, 1965.

Theophrastus. *De historia plantarum . . . Theodoro Gaza interprete.* Lyons, 1552.

Thomson, D. V. *The Schedula of Theophilus Presbyter.* Cambridge, 1932.

Traité de la peinture au pastel. Paris, 1788.

Bibliography

Trattato del disegno e della pittura: Aggiuntivi ancora i trattamenti sulla pittura, o sia la verissima maniera di divantare pittore in tre sole ore. Venice, 1768.

Udine, Jean d' [Albert Cozanet]. *De la corrélation des sons et des couleurs en l'art.* Paris, 1897.

———. *L'orchestration des couleurs: Analyse, classification et synthèse mathématique des sensations colorées.* Paris, 1903.

Viviani, Quirico. *Indicazioni per riconoscere il vero colore della porpora.* . . . Udine, Italy, 1931.

Wahl, André. *L'industrie des matières colorantes organiques.* Paris, 1912.

Watin, Jean-Félix. *Art du peintre, doreur et vernisseur . . . pour la fabrication et l'application des couleurs.* . . . 12th ed. Paris, 1864.

Way, A. " 'Mappia Clavicula," a Manuscript Treatise on the Preparation of Pigments and on the Various Processes of the Decorative Arts Practised during the Middle Ages." *Archaeologia* 32 (1847).

Weckerlin, Jean-Baptiste. *Le drap "escarlate" au Moyen-âge: Essai sur l'etymologie et la signification du mot écarlate et notes techniques sur la fabrication de ce drap de laine au Moyen-âge.* Lyons, 1905.

Wiley. H. W. *Influence of Artificial Colours on Digestion and Health.* Washington, D.C., 1904.

Wittgenstein, Ludwig. *Bemerkungen über die Farben.* Frankfurt, 1979. *Remarks on Color.* Translated by Linda L. McAliste and Margarete Schattle. Berkeley, Calif., 1977.